The 1921 Uprising in Malabar

The 1921 Uprising in Malabar

A Collection of Communist Writings

Edited by Nitheesh Narayanan and Vijay Prashad

First published in April 2022
Digital print edition, April 2022

LeftWord Books
2254/2A, Shadi Khampur
New Ranjit Nagar
New Delhi 110008
INDIA

LeftWord Books and Vaam Prakashan are imprints of
Naya Rasta Publishers Pvt. Ltd.

leftword.com

ISBN   978-93-92018-40-4 (paperback)
          978-93-92018-45-9 (e-book)

Contents

Acknowledgements   7

Contributors   9

Foreword
   Pinarayi Vijayan   11

Introduction
   Nitheesh Narayanan, Vijay Prashad   19

The Moplah Rising, 1922
   Abani Mukherji   49

Peasants Revolt in Malabar, 1921
   Saumyendranath Tagore   59

The Call and Warning of 1921
   Communist Party of India   75

The Moplah Rebellion
   E.M.S. Namboodiripad   79

The Direct Action Lessons of 1921
   A.K. Gopalan   94

Reflections on the Peasants' Revolt
   of 1921-22 in Malabar
   Subhashini Ali   104

Acknowledgements

Some spellings have been standardised across the book. For instance, the name of one of the most prominent leaders of the rebellion is spelt across the original writings variously as Wariankunnath Kunhammad Haji, Kunhahammed, Varian Kunnath Kunhahammad Haji, V. Kunhamed Haji, Kunha Ahmed Haji, Variankunnath Kunhamed Haji, Variath Kunhahammad Haji, Haji Kunhamad, Variath Kunhahammadaji, and Variyam Kunnath Kunhahammad Haji – we have used Wariankunnath Kunhammad Haji throughout, except in titles of articles or books, where the original form is retained.

We are grateful to Shilpa Shaji and Subin Dennis for their translations of some of these texts; to Devi Vijay for her splendid editing; to Abhinav (Political Popular) for the cover design; and to the team at LeftWord Books for speedily getting this book to press.

Contributors

ABANI MUKHERJI (1891-1937) was one of the founders of the Communist Party of India in 1920. He was a delegate to the 2nd (1920) and 3rd (1921) meetings of the Communist International as well as the Indian delegate to the Congress of the Peoples of the East, held in Baku (Soviet Republic), 1920. With M.N. Roy, Mukherji wrote the book *India in Transition* (1922), one of the first Marxist accounts of Indian history. Mukherji travelled to India as a courier of the Comintern and worked at the USSR's Academy of Sciences. He was killed in the purges of the 1930s.

A.K. GOPALAN (1904-1977), who cut his teeth in the Indian National Congress, joined the Congress Socialist Party in the 1930s and then became a key leader of the communist movement in India. He represented Cannanore (1952-57) and Kasaragod (1957-1971) in the Indian parliament, where he helped shape the role that communists must play in such an institution.

E.M.S. NAMBOODIRIPAD (1909-1998) was one of the founders of the Congress Socialist Party (1934) and played a key role in the freedom movement. He was Chief Minister of Kerala from 1957 to 1959 and from 1967 to 1969; he was the General Secretary of the Communist Party of India from 1962 to 1964 and of the Communist Party of India (Marxist) from 1978 to 1992. For his autobiography — *EMS Atmakatha* — he won the Sahithya Academy award in 1970.

NITHEESH NARAYANAN is a researcher at Tricontinental: Institute for Social Research, a PhD scholar from JNU, and the editor of *Student Struggle* (the journal of Students' Federation of India). He is a member of the central secretariat of the Students Federation of India. This is his first book in English.

PINARAYI VIJAYAN is Chief Minister of Kerala, a post he has held since May 2016. He is a member of the Politburo of the Communist Party of India (Marxist). He is the first chief minister of Kerala to be re-elected after serving a full term.

SAUMYENDRANATH TAGORE (1901-1974) was the first translator of the *Communist Manifesto* into Bengali; his translation was published in *Langal*, edited by Qazi Nazrul Islam. An early member of the Workers and Peasants Party, Tagore was an Indian delegate to the 6th Communist International meeting (1928). In 1934, Tagore broke with the Communist Party of India and formed the Communist League of India.

SUBHASHINI ALI is a Politburo member of the Communist Party of India (Marxist) and Vice-President of the All-India Democratic Women's Association (AIDWA).

VIJAY PRASHAD is the director of Tricontinental: Institute for Social Research, chief correspondent for Globetrotter, and an editor at LeftWord Books. His most recent books are *The Withdrawal: Iraq, Libya, Afghanistan, and the Fragility of US Power* (with Noam Chomsky), *Struggle Makes Us Human* (with Frank Barat), and *Selected Ho Chi Minh* (edited), all from LeftWord Books.

Foreword

Pinarayi Vijayan

During the 100th anniversary of the Malabar Rebellion, we heard something we have not heard for a hundred years. Some said that the Malabar Rebellion was not part of the freedom struggle and that the brave patriots who were part of the rebellion and had been killed by the British were not freedom fighters.

The Sangh Parivar is attempting to exclude the Malabar Rebellion from the history of the freedom struggle, to expel the true freedom fighters, to glorify those who had no role in the freedom struggle. This is an attempt to make the traitors brave and to fabricate a false history.

The uprising that took place in Eranad and Valluvanad Taluk, Malabar, in 1921 is known as the Malabar Rebellion. The British cast a communal frame on the struggle and branded it as the Mappilla (Muslims) riot. People like Muhammad Abdul Rahman, member of the Provincial Khalifat Committee (Kozhikode), viewed the struggle from a nationalist perspective and said that it should be called the Malabar Rebellion. On the 25th anniversary of the Malabar Rebellion, the Communist Party passed a resolution, *The Call and Warning*. The resolution highlighted the anti-British and anti-feudal character of this agrarian revolt. At the same time, it pointed out that there were weaknesses of the struggle and warned about the lessons that should be learned from such a struggle. Following the views of the British, the Malabar agrarian revolutionaries are now being kept out of the freedom struggle. The communal organisations now advocate that the Malabar Rebellion was to establish an Islamic state; these communal organisations support the British agenda of portraying the rebellion as the Mappila riot.

After the collapse of the Ottoman Empire, the British began to take over the caliphate's provinces in violation of their promise to the Caliph of Turkey. Muslims around the world fought against this British betrayal. This anti-British sentiment led to the Khilafat movement. The Khilafat movement and the nationalist movement fought together against Britain.

The atrocities of British imperialism and feudalism, the divisive tactics of Britain, the inhumane atrocities, the brave national consciousness of fighters such as Ali Musaliyar and Wariankunnath, the content of the agrarian rebellion, the anti-British nature irrespective of religion, and the history embraced by the warriors are being rejected by those fabricating a fake history.

During the rebellion, there was a joint strike committee. K.P. Keshav Menon, Moidhu Moulavi, K. Madhavan Nair, Ali Musaliyar, Wariankunnath Kunhammad Haji, and Chembrasseri Thangal were part of this committee; there was no religious segregation. In 1920, Maulana Shaukat Ali and Gandhiji visited Kozhikode together. These all are historical facts. Now there are efforts to distort and rewrite them. The strengthening of Hindu-Muslim unity through the peasant struggle became a major fuel for the Malabar Rebellion. That, too, is being disregarded.

The attempt of the Sangh Parivar to communalise the Malabar riots is not something new. Now, however, these attempts are endorsed by the Indian Council of Historical Research. The Malabar Rebellion is portrayed as a mere communal conflict. The Sangh Parivar narrative that the rebellion was a religious struggle fundamentally aimed at establishing a theocratic state has also been echoed from some other corners.

It is undeniable that the agitation in Malabar started as part of the nationwide freedom struggle organised by the Congress and the Khilafat in 1921. Unlike other parts of India, the agitation in Eranad and Valluvanad developed an anti-feudal character. The British sought to transform the feudal structure favourable for colonial exploitation. They aimed to bring the feudal landlords under their dominance and turn them into their supporters. The new landlords implemented anti-people measures. The British backed all such measures. British rule legalised landlordism and gave more powers to the landlord.

Since the natural resources had become the private property of the hegemonic powers, large-scale foreign capital-based activities took place. When such a situation arose, great repercussions struck the region. Conflicts erupted in many places. When these conflicts caused problems for the government, the District Collector William Logan was appointed as Special Commissioner in February 1881 to investigate the 'land tenure system and the tenants' land, and the sites for the churches and grave plans'. Logan's report of 1882 was based on his studies of the thousands of petitions and the district records. Logan's report pointed out that the policy adopted by the British in Malabar from the very beginning in matters relating to the possession of land was flawed, that the act of recognising the landlord as the principal owner of the land and giving him the right to enjoy a large share of the crops produced on the land at will, was the result of a reckless and exorbitant lease. He also described all forms of oppression, such as extortion and indiscriminate evictions.

The investigation by the Revenue Board member Victor Botham in 1886 found that poverty and discontent among tenants were reasons for the riots. In other words, in Malabar, especially in Eranad and Valluvanad regions, poverty and land-related issues caused great dissatisfaction among the people. A large section of the tenants was Muslims. The British portrayed the discontent in a communal light. Muslims were not the only ones who lined up in the conflict that arose over agrarian issues. Non-Muslims were also involved in the Wagon Tragedy. Tenants such as Kunnappally

Achuthan Nair and Meledath Sankaran Nair, and wage labourers such as Kizhakkipalathil Thattan Unni Kurayan and Chorakarambayil Chettichiku were killed in the Wagon Tragedy.

As the rebels advanced into the anti-British struggle, the British who had defended feudalism received aid from the landlords. The British, the landlords, and pro-British activists stood against the revolt. Thus, the revolt grew into an anti-British and anti-feudal movement and agitation against the British agents.

In a letter to the Chief Secretary on 7 January 1881, Willian Logan warned that 'whatever the relationship between landlord and tenant in this area, it is rapidly moving towards a crisis stage'. At this juncture, the Khilafat movement came to prominence with its anti-British slogans.

Mozhikunnath Brahmadhan Namboodiripad was arrested as part of the riots in Cherpulassery at the beginning of the Khilafat uprising and was tortured in a British prison for a long time. After the revolt, he wrote in his autobiography,

> Communal strife is not the root cause of this rebellion. It originates from political oppression, and police brutality triggered this unrest. This rebellion was only a part of the freedom struggle. When the freedom struggle was intensifying, a section of the people abandoned their discipline as the result of police intrusion leading to the unfortunate incident. As they slipped out of control, others, too, felt insecure. They were also subjected to police brutality.

It is a fact that as the agitations spread, unfair practices arose in some places. Pointing to such problems, the Communist Party said there were some warnings in the 1921 uprising. But it cannot be forgotten that leaders like Wariankunnath were keen to tackle such tendencies. Madhavan Nair, who strongly opposed the violent approach of the rebellion, in his book titled *Malabar Rebellion*, describes how Wariankunnath had reacted when he pointed out the wrongdoings of the rebellion. 'If I find any Mappila plundering, I will cut off his right hand. No doubt about it. I came here learning that a robbery had taken place'. These are the words of Wariankunnath.

Sardar Chandroth quoted Kunhahammad Haji's speech in *Deshabhimani* on 25 August 1946:

It is being said in foreign countries that this is a war between Hindus and Muslims. But if they help the government or betray the people for the government, they will be ruthlessly punished. If I find out someone insulting Hindus unnecessarily, I will punish them. Hindus are our natives. We do not want to make it a Muslim country.

Where is the communal attitude in these words?

It is clear that he dreamt of a system in which all believers could live; he did not want to create an Islamic state. Kunhahammad Haji named his land Malayalanadu.

The letter written by Wariankunnath to the *Hindu* detailing the real face of the revolt is a historical document. It says pro-British Hindus faced problems. Wariankunnath did not show any sympathy for the pro-British Muslims either. Police officers like Amusahib and Moitheen Circle were killed. Chekkutty Adhikari from Anakkayam was beheaded for betrayal, and a procession was made with his speared head. The history books show that the rebels reached the home of Kondotty Thangal. Would this have happened if communalism was the content of the rebellion?

E. Moythumoulavi was imprisoned for two and a half years for his participation in the Khilafat movement. He made it clear that the rebels clashed with all those who had helped the British. Moulavi stated that the Moplahs 1921 encounter with the British government was not their first, and that the rebellion had not jolted Hindu-Muslim harmony in Malabar. He also explained that Muslims guarded many Hindu homes:

The Kottakal Kovilakam was guarded by about a hundred Muslims under the leadership of Odaya Purathu Chekutty Sahib, a native of Kalpakancherry and not a single stick was damaged by the rebellion. They also guarded the palace of the Warriers at Kottakal.

Such incidents show that the rebels took a strong stand against the pro-British people, regardless of religion, while the leaders, including Wariankunnath, took a similar stance regarding misconduct in some places.

These are the facts. This is history. However, both the Sangh Parivar and the Islamic nationalists have used the same British propaganda to obscure the actual role of the rebels.

If we look at the agrarian struggles, it can be seen that the struggles began from many impulses. Later, the Communists developed those views in the right direction. The communists carried out the struggle against imperialism and feudalism. The Kayyur martyrs — four Communists whom the British executed for their role in the peasant movement — chanted slogans against feudalism and imperialism. When the Communist Party took over the struggle, they replaced erroneous methods. At the same time, they had a clear vision of creating equality.

Distorting the country's history is an essential part of the Sangh Parivar agenda. They are preparing to create a Hindu nation by destroying India's Renaissance tradition and undermining its democratic, secular, and socialist foundations. The biggest obstacle to formulating ideas for that is the country's history. The onslaught on the Malabar Rebellion is now part of a broader plan to make the new generation blind to our history, erase the Renaissance values from our brains, and create the attitude they need.

Communists have understood this plan. This injustice to history should not be forgiven. The Communists had conceived Malabar Rebellion as a call and a warning as they were doing justice to history. There is no doubt that the Muslim masses, who entered the movement as part of the freedom struggle and the tenant movement, also had feelings of Islamic brotherhood. EMS himself explains this in his book *Communist Party in Kerala*.

The British imprisoned A.K. Gopalan, popularly known as AKG, for his words: 'Whether you are a Hindu or a Muslim. If you are anti-imperialist and want the British rule to end, you must learn the lesson of the courageous struggle of the patriotic youth in 1921. Without it, you cannot end British rule'. AKG gave this speech on 25 August 1946, the 25th anniversary of the Malabar Struggle. Though all political prisoners were released after independence, AKG was not released. It was decided to proceed with the case. AKG filed a petition in court against this. 'The sacrifice and courage of the Khilafat Mappilas in 1921 are commendable, and if calling for the acceptance of the good parts of the struggle and warning them to guard against the bad aspects is a guilt, then I am guilty', AKG said in the petition. The court acquitted AKG. That is the position of the communists.

Now the Sangh Parivar and their accomplices are trying to erase the Malabar riots from history by using the same arguments and phrases of the British. Their foot soldiers still follow the strategy of British imperialism to divide and rule India through such approaches.

At this stage, we have a responsibility to prevent attacks on history and present the true face of those at the helm to the public. The lesson before us is that we must be vigilant throughout society.

Introduction

Nitheesh Narayanan, Vijay Prashad

In 1921-22, a hundred years ago, the people of Kerala's Malabar region revolted. The slogans on the lips of the agriculturalists who conducted this uprising circled around agrarian distress caused by the heavy hand of imperialism. Twenty years later, the communist poet Kambalath Govindan Nair, one of the early leaders of the teacher's movement in Kerala, sang:

Nammalundakkunna nellu
janmimaare theetuvaan
Sammathikkillennathaanu
hethu etumuttuvaan
Nammalute kaashuvaangim-
glandilekkayakkuvaan
Sammathikkillennathaanu
hethu etumuttuvaan

Reason for our fight:
Our objection to
feeding the lords
with our rice.
Reason for our fight:
Our objection to
sending our assets
to England.

Nitheesh Narayanan, Vijay Prashad

BRITISH IMPERIALISM, JENMI LANDLORDS, AND
THE RESENTMENT OF THE TENANTS

Two elements constituted the structure of Malabar agriculture: British imperialism, which set in place this structure in 1792 when the British took over direct control over Malabar and which absorbed the bulk of the region's social surplus, and the Jenmis, the landlords whose absolute control over the land had been established by the British. The British overlords reversed whatever reforms the tenants (*Verumpatakkaran*), mainly Muslims but also oppressed caste *Thiyyas*, had been able to wrest from the regime of Tipu Sultan (Sultan of Mysore from 1782-1799). Tenant unrest — mainly among the Muslims (referred to in the Malabar region as the Moplahs) — did not wait 129 years. The first rebellion of the Moplahs took place as early as 1836. It was crushed, but the violence against the tenants did not prevent a string of lesser protests throughout the 19th century. These continued protests suggest why the British continued to investigate resentment amongst the Moplahs (such as the Malabar Special Commission, 1881-82, headed by William Logan), why they passed a series of laws to both ameliorate the tenants' condition and to punish them (The Moplah Outrages Act, 1855 and the Malabar Compensation for Tenants Improvement Act, 1887), and why they had to deal with the murder or attempted murder of British colonial officials by the tenants (Henry Valentine Conolly, the Collector, killed in 1855, and Charles Alexander Innes, the settlement officer, who survived an attack in 1915).

British policy from 1792 produced a landlord class that was almost god-like. Their paramountcy went uncriticised as long as they provided a substantial tax to the British coffers in a timely fashion. The landlords had the power to charge whatever rent they wished to fulfil the British demands, and they had the right to evict any tenant at any time. Logan's report details that the evictions of tenants increased between 1860 and 1880, partly due to the increase in British demands. His suggestion to fix tenancy came from the best liberal tradition, except it was impossible as long as British colonialism imposed a heavy tax on the landlords, who used their latitude to extract rack-rents from the peasantry. Neither the 1887 act nor the 1900 act, which nominally put in place some protections for the tenants, had any bearing on the actual violence of the landlords against the tenants. The long history of protest in the Malabar region is related in kind to the long history of protests in the subcontinent against British imperialism's agrarian policy: from the Santhal Hul (1855) and the Nil Bidroha (1859) in Bengal to the Deccan Riots (1875) in the high plateau in central and southern India.

Understanding the power of tenant resentment, the British — as early as 1836 — began to describe these uprisings, not in class but in religious terms. In the Malabar region, the tenants were mainly Muslims, and the landlords were Hindus; the small number of oppressed caste tenants, including *Cheruman* serfs, converted to Islam in the 19th century. The British called the protests 'outrages' and spent a hundred years trying to suppress them using violence and sowing the seeds of religious discord between the (Hindu) landlords and the (Muslim) tenants. Judge Thomas Lumisden Strange's special commission (1852) rejected the possibility that agrarian distress had created the basis for the uprisings; the reason was to be found in 'fanaticism', a word laden with anti-Muslim meaning.[1] That is why the British passed the Moplah Outrages Acts, which allowed the Malabar Police — created to control the tenants — to arrest anyone with a 'war knife', confiscate tenant's property, and deport tenants. Not every British official agreed with this view. The Collector of Malabar, Atholl Macgregor, wrote in 1874, 'Fanaticism is merely the instrument through which the terrorism of the landed classes is

---

[1] Judge T. L. Strange, Minute no. 123, 17 February 1852, p/327/44, MJP, p. 678. Conrad Wood, 'The Moplah Rebellion of 1921-1922 and Its Genesis', London: University of London, Ph.D., 1975, p. 34.

aimed at'. F. Fawcett, the superintendent of police in Malabar and an anthropologist, noted in 1897 that the colonial State developed a land tenure system 'such as if arranged specially for the purpose of making people discontented'.[2] But Macgregor and Fawcett (as well as William Logan, who wrote the 1887 *Malabar Manual*) were in the minority. The majority view — and therefore the view of the colonial State — was that any outbreak was fanaticism rooted in Islam and that these outbreaks did not require negotiation or reform but only violence by the colonial State.

In his important contribution on the Malabar Revolt (collected in this book), Communist leader E.M.S. Namboodiripad captured the colonial State's lingering worry about rebellion and its refusal to address the root cause of the unrest. To establish that this was not merely a problem of Malabar, EMS compared the colonial State's response in this case to that of its much longer colonial presence in Ireland. 'Sufficient to say that the Malabar tenancy question was as recurrent and persistent a subject in Madras for half a century as the Irish question was (for four centuries) in London. And yet its solution did not touch the fringe of the problem even as the Anglo-Irish treaty has not touched the fringe of the British colonial problem'. The British colonial State could only answer the Irish Question with violence. It was the same in Malabar. That is why EMS, wrote, the people in both Ireland and Malabar had to fight against the intractable nature of the colonial State and its economic system. It was the popular struggle that forced the colonial State in both instances to settle partly the contradictions between its theft and the suffering of the people:

What is more, the solution of the tenancy question in 1930 had to be preceded by the Rebellion of 1921 even as the settlement of the Irish question in 1921 had to be preceded by the Easter Rising of 1916. We will, therefore, now refer to

---

[2] F. Fawcett, 'The Moplahs of Malabar', *Imperial and Asiatic Quarterly Review,* vol. IV, October 1897, p. 296.

this historic rising which was the fiercest struggle against the British authority since 1857.

Nair's poem explicitly rejected the British colonial view and pointed directly toward the underlying cause of the long history of unrest in Malabar: British imperialism and Jenmi landlordism.

MALABAR AND THE FREEDOM MOVEMENT.

In 1920, the Congress held its fifth District Conference in Manjeri (Eranad taluk, Malabar). At this meeting, the organisers formed the Kerala Provincial Congress Committee. The national debate between those who wanted full self-government (Extremists) and those who wanted just a little more home rule (Moderates) was mirrored in Manjeri, where the Extremists took over the Congress Committee. The Congress had been largely dominated by dominant castes (Nairs, but also some Namboodiri Brahmins), whose professions included *kanamdars* (large tenants) and *vakils* (lawyers). The 1920 Congress transformed the local organisation due to several factors: by the entry of Moplahs through MK Gandhi's urging unity with the Khilafat movement (to reinstate the Turkish Sultan as the Caliph of the Muslim world) and by the fact that the Congress took place in a largely Moplah town.

Gandhi and Khilafat leader Shaukat Ali came to Calicut in August 1920 to speak about non-cooperation and Khilafat, with Gandhi making a powerful plea for united action against British imperialism:

I consider the eternal friendship between the Hindus and Mussulmans is more important than the British connection. I would prefer any day anarchy and chaos in India to an armed peace brought about by the bayonet between the Hindus and Mussulmans. I have therefore ventured to suggest to my Hindu brethren that if they wanted to live at peace with Mussulmans, there is an opportunity which is not going to recur for the next hundred years.[3]

The colonial State was aware that the unity championed by Gandhi had produced results, linking people such as P. Moideen Koya of the Moplahs with local Congress leaders such as K. Madhavan Nair, U. Gopala Menon, and P. Achuthan. In January 1921, the highest religious authority of the Moplahs — *Mahadum Tangal* of Ponnani — held a meeting that pledged Moplah support to the Congress' non-cooperation movement.[4] Many Moplah leaders began a boycott of foreign goods and colonial institutions so that many resigned from their jobs in the colonial State. It was already clear to the British colonial State that the stirrings were not religious but oriented by the agrarian question (District Collector E. F. Thomas wrote in January 1921 that the Moplah masses were 'much more interested in the tenants' movement, and the agitators can't get a hearing unless they make tenancy questions the big cry').[5]

The idea of *swaraj* (independence) swept through the region. The revolt seized Eranad and Valluvanad from the colonial State and declared them as independent regions, an independence that lasted for three months. The revolt led to attacks against British colonial officials. The people abolished the tax system, destroyed government documents that documented the debt of the peasantry, issued a new passport, and treated the territory as sovereign by the people irrespective of their religion. In his fortnightly report, the Governor of Madras, the 1st Marquess of Willingdon, wrote that the All-India Khilafat Conference held at Karachi had 'produced

---

[3] M. K. Gandhi, 'Speech at Calicut' (18 August 1920), *Collected Works*, vol. 21, p. 183.

[4] Robert Hardgrave, 'The Mapilla Rebellion 1921: Peasant Revolt in Malabar', *Modern Asian Studies*, II, I, 1977, p 67.

[5] E. F. Thomas, 'A Note on Events in Malabar in 1921', G. R. F. Tottenham (editor), *The Mapilla Rebellion*, 1921-22, Madras: Government Press, 1922, p. 4.

an impression on the mind of the Mappilla [Moplah] that the end of the British Raj is at hand. It is certainly true that as a result of Khilafat propaganda, the Mappillas are better organised than they used to be and also better informed as to the strength of their own position and the difficulty of taking military action against them'.[6] Amongst the rebels were veterans of the Indian forces, who had served in the imperial forces in Iraq in 1920. Fresh from combat, they brought these skills to the uprising. Willingdon was tense because of the wildly popular Malabar rebellion — with soldiers in their midst — and because of the strike of 10,000 workers in the Buckingham and Carnatic mills that ran from June 1921 to October 1921, paralysing the economy of Madras. By August 1921, the colonial officials were 'satisfied from reports received that a state of open rebellion exists'.[7] Both the Malabar rebellion and the working-class strike had to be crushed.

The press of the landlords and aristocrats of Kerala — *Malayala Manorama* — sniffed the air and smelled Revolution.

It has been established that it is impossible to rein in the ignorant people after they have been encouraged to defy the established administration. The Bolshevik leaders told the people of Russia that heaven-like fortune would come to them if they sabotaged the existing regime; now they face indescribable hardships. . . . Following the famous French Revolution, the adversities faced by the French and the world are indescribable. This was after people were advised to rise so that the King could be driven out and the influence of the aristocrats eliminated; they believed that their sufferings would be removed.[8]

---

[6] Governor of Madras, Fortnightly Report to the Viceroy , 17 August 1921, Tottenham, *The Mapilla Rebellion*, p. 12.

[7] Hardgrave, 'The Mapilla Rebellion 1921', p. 85.

[8] 'Malabarile Lahala', *Malayala Manorama*, 25 August 1921.

As far as the editors of the landlords' paper felt, the Malabar Rebellion could escalate into something like the French or the Russian revolutions. This was not to be permitted. The landlords and the aristocrats would support anything — even terrible violence from the colonial State — to prevent such an outcome.

District Collector E. F. Thomas authorised the entry of troops and the Malabar Police into the town of Tirurangadi, where they used armed force to arrest people and then — controversially — fired on a crowd and surrounded the Mambaram Mosque. According to Mohammad Abdul Rahman of the Provincial Khilafat Committee in Calicut, the mood in the crowd was of 'insurrection'.[9] The Malayalam press that was incensed by the shooting called Thomas the 'Dyer of Malabar', associating him with Colonel Reginald Dyer, who had led his soldiers to massacre thousands of peaceful protestors in Amritsar's Jallianwala Bagh on 13 April 1919. General John Burnett-Stuart, who oversaw the crackdown in the Malabar region, wrote to Army Headquarters (Pune), 'I cannot commit myself to any prophesy as to when the rebellion can be expected to end. It may go in some districts until every Moplah is either exterminated or arrested'. It is not accidental that extermination came to his mind before arrest. The horror was made clear when seventy prisoners asphyxiated on a train to Bellary (this incident is known as the Wagon Tragedy). The key government of India report for 1922 — *Moral and Material Progress and Condition of India* — noted that the rebellion and the use of force against it 'brought home to many people the ultimate dependence of law and order upon the military arm'.[10]

Meanwhile, the colonial State and sections of the Malabar landlord class characterised the revolt as solely religious. Of course, as the rebellion unfolded, there were recorded cases of peasant violence against the landlords that had both a class and

[9] Hardgrave, 'The Mapilla Rebellion 1921', p. 79.
[10] *Statement exhibiting the Moral and Material Progress and Condition of India During the Year 1921*, no. 57, New Delhi: Government Press, 1922, p. 18.

a religious character. Such rebellions do not draw within the lines since they develop out of the concrete and complex identities of those who rebel. But to reduce the rebellion to sectarianism or religion misses key aspects of the class nature of the uprising. There was no major difference in the coverage of the *Madras Mail* (the colonial paper) and *Malayala Manorama* (the landlord paper) since both blamed the revolt on the work of 'ignorant and fanatic Muslims'. British propaganda not only shaped the narrative about the uprising in 1921-22 but — as Pinarayi Vijayan says in the foreword — has remained part of the contemporary thinking driven by the Hindutva forces.

The contradictions of history led the dominant caste Hindus to fear that the Moplah rebellion was merely the harbinger of more revolts, perhaps against Brahmanical patriarchy and the wretchedness of the caste system. After the colonial State crushed the 1921-22 revolt, the dominant caste Hindu leaders gathered for a meeting. Mannargat Muppil Nair, one of the leading landlords of Malabar, presided over the gathering. The meeting passed several resolutions, including one on the patriarchal marriage system that existed specifically amongst dominant caste Hindus. These leaders acknowledged that some reforms had to be conceded otherwise discontent would grow within the ranks of the Hindus. That is the reason why they asked for these reforms within the Madras Marriage Act.[11]

One significant resolution was about the oppressed castes. It is important to note that in various parts of Malabar, but particularly in the southern region, many Moplahs had come from the oppressed caste communities of *Cherumans*, *Mukkuvans*, and *Thiyyas*; they abandoned their oppressed status by becoming Muslims. The resolution of the caste Hindu leaders read, 'Whereas the elevation of the depressed classes has become indispensable for the existence of Hindu society, and whereas infusing of a sense

---

[11] 'Awakened Malabar. Lessons of the rebellion', *Times of India*, 22 June 1922.

of self-respect into them is a condition precedent to any sort of elevation, all that is necessary to make the Depressed Classes self-respective must be done immediately'.[12] It is important to point out that these caste Hindu leaders operated under the assumption that all Hindus — irrespective of their castes — belonged to a community. If this Hindu community remained suffocatingly hierarchical, then more oppressed castes might abandon it for other religions. The communal thought of the caste Hindu leaders was that they needed to retain the oppressed castes even as they maintained the essence of the hierarchies (this was known as *sangathan*). Reform in these orthodox Hindu camps was not motivated by human feeling; it was driven by hatred of Muslims.

It is worth noting here that one of the key leaders of the Moplahs, Wariankunnath Kunhammad Haji, said during the rebellion:

No one should be starved. The haves should give money to the have-nots if they ask. If not, they will have to face stringent punishment. No one should harass the *Cherumakkals* [Dalits].[13]

The landlords' assessment was adopted by Gandhi and Congress leadership. They feared the revolutionary currents and preferred the communal narrative to the realities of the class struggle. Moyarath Sankaran, who was a member of the Congress at the time of the uprising and later joined the Communist movement, recalled his disappointment with the Congress leadership two decades later.

The Malabar peasant struggle was, from beginning to end, a huge movement against the British administration. At no point

---

[12] 'Awakened Malabar. Lessons of the rebellion', *Times of India*, 22 June 1922.
[13] Sardar Chandroth, 'Kunhammed Haji: Brave Moplah Leader', *Deshabhimani*, 25 August 1946.

in time was it a Hindu-Muslim clash. What upset Congress workers like us was the fact that even Gandhiji did not see through the machinations of the British towards the peasant struggle by wilfully giving it a communal colouring, labelling it as a Hindu-Muslim clash, and causing it to be ridiculed in newspaper reports.[14]

Some Muslims, Sankaran suggested, operated as agents of the colonial State, and it was these agents that attacked Hindu homes and families to paint the uprising with a communal brush. The acts of such agent provocateurs discredited the Khalifat movement and the peasant uprising.

HOW THE COMMUNISTS UNDERSTOOD
THE MOPLAH REBELLION

Communist writing on the Moplah Rebellion has consistently questioned the communal narratives deployed by the British, the landlords and the aristocrats, and the forces of Hindutva. This volume collects six of the definitive Communist voices from 1921 to 2021 that challenge the attempt to communalise the Moplah Rebellion; instead, they offer fact-based, materialist analyses that foregrounds the class character of the agrarian revolts, the way in which class intersects with other social identities (of religion and caste) in the unfurling of the rebellion, and the national and international shape of the rebellion. The early communists and some secular nationalists understood the rebellion to have a class character, but which would be manifest — due to the land tenure system set in place in Malabar — with religious and caste characteristics.

In October 1921, the communist Abani Mukherji wrote a report on the Moplah rebellion. Mukherji was one of the early

---

[14] Moyarath Sankaran, *Autobiography of a Freedom Fighter and Martyr,* Trivandrum: Chintha Publishers, 2016.

members of the Communist Party of India (CPI), founded in 1920 at Tashkent, USSR. His report is perhaps the first that emphasises the class character of the rebellion. He closed his text with sharpness:

> The Hindus suffered most from the wrath of the insurgents, not because they were of a different religion from these, but because most of the oppressors were Hindus. In the interests of the bourgeois, the Moplahs have been shot down by machine guns, but the Government has succeeded in suppressing by this slaughter the revolutionary sentiments of the poor peasants and workmen of India.

Lenin read Mukherji's report in November 1921 and sent it to Nikolai Bukharin of the Communist International (Comintern) with a note:

> Please read this. We need to have (regardless of this particular article, which, however, appears to be good) more publications of Indian comrades in order to encourage them and to collect more information about India and her revolutionary movement.[15]

Mukherji's text was published in *Die Internationale*, *The Communist Review*, and other journals, and circulated within the Comintern. Lenin's perspicacity to identify that this rebellion indicated the possible revolutionary energy of the Indian masses illuminates two points: first, Lenin's understanding of the Indian situation, since there was already ongoing a massive strike wave of workers and a series of peasant rebellions, and second, Lenin's ability to understand that beneath the surface of the struggle — which had religious overtones — there were complex class realities

---

[15] Lenin to Bukharin, 14 November 1921, *Collected Works*, vol. 45, p. 376.

at work that had to be foregrounded by a political formation of the people.

While working on this report, Abani Mukherji assisted MN Roy, a leading communist at that time, on *India in Transition*, one of the first Marxist books to appear on the Indian reality. In this book, Roy and Mukherji focused attention on the agrarian crisis in India since 'the economic position of the peasantry was becoming absolutely hopeless'.[16] Due to this, they saw evidence — since 1917 — in Bihar, the United Provinces, and the Malabar region, of the revolutionary capacity of the peasantry, a capacity far beyond the bourgeois anti-colonialism of Gandhi. 'The peasantry is revolting', they wrote, and while the peasantry has revolted over the past century, 'the agrarian trouble has assumed an acute and wide-spread aspect in the national life of the country'.[17] Here is their general assessment of the political situation in the Indian countryside:

Since 1918, the peasant movement in the north of the country has become a standing affair. Local risings and riots are very frequent and of such a serious nature that the military is often called in to cope with the situation. Appreciating the potentiality of the agrarian movement, the Indian National Congress admitted in its session of 1916 a great number of peasant delegates. But the bourgeois political movement has demonstrated its utter inability to understand as well as to lead the agrarian movement. In the winter of 1920, the agrarian movement broke out in the most violent form; it almost assumed the proportions of an insurrection. This happened in the province of Oudh, where the Zamindari system prevails, and the power of the landholders is very extensive. The peasants' actions were well organised; they

[16] M.N. Roy and Abani Mukerji, *India in Transition*, Geneva: JB Target, 1922, p. 85.
[17] Roy and Mukherji, *India in Transition*, p. 84.

were directed only against the rich landholders, until the government sent troops to protect their lives and properties. Houses were burned, estates looted, and crops destroyed by the rioters. The immediate cause of this serious outbreak had been the highhanded methods with which the Talukdars (big landholders) extracted from the cultivators the large sums of money which the former had contributed to the war fund in the previous years. This made the already heavy economic burden, caused by excessive taxation, and rise of prices, unbearable for the poor peasants. Of course, the government rushed to the aid of the propertied class and crushed the revolt with military force. But the movement has not died; on the contrary it is steadily spreading to other parts. These agrarian disturbances have, during the course of the last year, crystallised into a political movement.[18]

A brief section that follows this assessment is specifically on the Malabar Rebellion. It draws from the report by Abani Mukherji but links it to the general peasant unrest that opened in Champaran (Bihar) and Kheda (Gujarat) in 1917:

The latest phase of the agrarian trouble is the Moplah risings on the coast of Malabar. Subsequent information shows that the movement has been advancing to the east coast as well. The Moplahs are the descendants of the Arab traders who came to India centuries ago. Their number does not exceed a million. They are very poor, agriculture being their means of livelihood, and have always been under the thumb of the moneylenders, who are Hindus. The majority of the big landholders in that part of the country also happen to be Hindu. The recent revolt is caused by purely economic causes. It was started by looting the houses of the landholders and

---

[18] Roy and Mukherji, *India in Transition*, pp. 86-87.

moneylenders, with a demand for remission of rent and for getting back the land that had been concentrating in the hands of the speculator and capitalist agents. But in every instance of peasant disturbance the government promptly demonstrates its class affiliation by rendering military aid to the landholders; thus, the class differentiation of Indian society is brought into evidence for those who care to see it. The Zamindars and landholders may struggle with the government to maintain their privileged position, unchanged by the new economic policy of the latter; and the government may 'protect' the cultivator from the abuses committed by the Zamindar; but as soon as the peasant revolts against the system that starves him to death, he finds the ranks closed in the enemy camp. Such is the social and economic position of the agricultural population of India. It stands between two classes of exploiter viz, 1. the foreign capitalists and 2. native landholder, usurer, and trader. The two may disagree and struggle about the share each should have in the exploitation, but both of them are identical in their fundamental social significance — they live and thrive on the labour of the toiler, be he a worker in the factory or cultivator of the soil.[19]

By the time *India in Transition* was published, rebellions of this kind spread across India — from the peasant rebellion in Awadh (1921-22) to the Manyam Rebellion near the Godavari River in Andhra (1922-24). During the heated phase of unrest across India, the colonial State, the emergent Hindu right-wing, and bourgeois sections of the Congress attempted to make the case that these protests were somehow illegitimate. It was easier to deal with them as a law-and-order problem, whether occasioned by criminality or by religious warfare. In this context, the early communist writings highlighted the class component of the struggles, perhaps, even

---

[19] Roy and Mukherji, *India in Transition*, pp. 87-88.

exaggerating it a little in the face of the political role of religious and caste bonds. This emphasis on the class assessment is there in Abani Mukerji's report (1921), which opens this volume. Fifteen years later, Saumyendranath Tagore, the first to translate the *Communist Manifesto* into Bengali, toured the country on behalf of the Communist League of India. These travels included a visit to the Malabar region, where Tagore — the grand-nephew of Rabindranath Tagore — closely studied the rebellion and then wrote a powerful report about it in 1937, collected in this volume.

In April 1943, E.M.S. Namboodiripad wrote a very sharp history of the peasant movement in Kerala for the Kisan Sabha.[20] Here, EMS provided an analysis of the Malabar uprising that accepted the general view of Abani Mukherji and Saumyendranath Tagore about the class character of the uprising, but then asked one very important question:

> Why was it that the movement was confined to an area with a Moplah majority? . . . The oppression and exploitation of the Jenmi and the officials are as bad for the Hindu peasants as for their Moplah comrades. Why is it then that the Moplah peasants rose almost to a man while the Hindu peasants fell victim to the propaganda that the rising was not anti-Jenmi or anti-government but anti-Hindu.

EMS offered some observations that require careful thought:

1. The Moplah peasants are better organised than the Hindu peasants. 'Their congregational prayers, their common feasts and dinners, their conception of equality among themselves, etc., make them much more amenable to organised work than their brethren of other communities'.

---

[20] E.M.S. Namboodiripad, 'A Short History of the Peasant Movement in Kerala', *History, Society, and Land Relations. Selected Essays*, New Delhi: LeftWord Books, 2010.

2. The Khilafat call held an emotive power for the Moplahs. For the Hindu peasants, EMS wrote, the uprising was 'a question of freedom from bureaucracy and the Jenmi', but for the Moplah peasantry it was 'a question of defending [their] religious head, a question of sacred war against the desecrator of [their] creed'.

3. In the course of the rebellion, elements of these first two points revealed themselves and produced tensions not only along class, but also along community lines. EMS notes that in the initial phase, the leadership of the Congress — mostly the 'typical bourgeois nationalist leadership' of lawyers and intellectuals 'drawn from among the kanamdars' — called for a non-violent agitation against the landlord; when the masses began to 'adopt their own method of struggle' — namely outside the 'creed of nonviolence' — then, this leadership 'left them to their fate'. It was immediately clear to EMS that the 'Moplah elements of the same leadership' — such as Mohammed Abdur Rahman — stood for the *verumpattamdars* and therefore were 'more progressive', staying with the struggle through its course. The local-level leadership, EMS wrote, 'consisted mainly of Musaliars, Thangals, Hajis, and other saintly Moplahs'. These people were, he noted, 'sincere anti-imperialists', but they 'think and speak in the terms of religion which had tremendous effect in rallying the Moplahs'. If there were a principled central leadership, these anti-imperialists would have become important organisers. 'Their loss is irreparable to the peasant movement', since they drifted further into religious rather than class politics.

EMS's assessment in 1943 cautioned against too hasty a dismissal of the religious character of the movement and an exaggeration of its class character, although to be fair to both

Mukerji and Tagore, neither neglected the tendency toward communalism driven by opportunistic sections.

In 1946, at the 25th anniversary of the Malabar Rebellion, the debate about how to characterise it sharpened. The colonial and Hindu right-wing view of this being a communal riot hardened, while the Communist approach was much clearer. The Communist Party of India's newspaper *Deshabhimani* published many articles that contributed to the debate. Sardar Chandroth (1900-1964), who had been the head of the Malabar District Congress Committee and then who joined the CPI, wrote an article that quoted extensively from the Moplah leader, Wariankunnath Kunjahammed Haji:

> We have no hatred towards Hindus. But those who help the government and those who betrayed us to the government will be punished mercilessly. If it is known that somebody harms Hindus unnecessarily, I will punish them. Hindus are our fellow countrymen. We have no wish to make this a Muslim country.[21]

Evidence that many of the Moplahs went into this rebellion with awareness of the possibility of religious polarisation was important to highlight, particularly since the Hindu right-wing wanted to characterise the event as a pogrom against Hindus. Our volume ends with an essay by Subhashini Ali, whose family was directly impacted by the rebellion, protected by the Moplah rebels against communal elements who opportunistically wanted to use the energy of the uprising for their narrow ends.

In 1946, the CPI passed a resolution — collected in this volume — which assessed the rebellion based on its class character without erasing its social content. There are many key points raised in the resolution, but we wanted to highlight one of them, namely

---

[21] Sardar Chandroth, 'Kunhahammed Haji: Brave Moplah Leader', *Deshabhimani*, 25 August 1946.

that the resolution notes that the brutality of the asphyxiation of the Moplahs in the Wagon Tragedy 'can only be compared to the barbarism of Hitler-fascism'. This assertion that fascist actions took place in the colonies, and that it was 'barbarism' anticipates Aimé Césaire's tremendous book, *Discourse on Colonialism* (1950), which shows that Hitler's brutality in Europe is merely what the colonisers had done in the colonies.

Shortly after the 1921 rebellion, K. P. Kesava Menon, the Congress leader, founded a newspaper *Mathrubhumi*, which he edited for fifty years. When the CPI published its resolution, *Mathrubhumi* responded with a sharp attack.[22] EMS responded with the following article in *Deshabhimani:*

The resolution of Communist party, published in *Deshabhimani* has become a topic for an editorial in *Mathrubhumi*. *Mathrubhumi* argues that the resolution threatens to provoke a communal riot, such as it says happened in 1921 and the one that happened recently in Calcutta.

Anyone who reads the resolution will say that this allegation is baseless. The title of the resolution of the Communist Party is 'The Call and Warning'. The resolution praises the anti-British character of the 1921 rebellion and gives a warning against its communal character. The reader can see both these from the beginning to the end of the resolution. Even without an appeal, the people know that they should enter into the anti-British struggle, such as the struggle in 1921. The people do not trust the commitment of Wavell, Cripps, and C. P. Ramaswami Aiyyar, people that the *Mathrubhumi* editor and other Congress leaders trust.

The autocrats in British India and in the princely states are brutally oppressing the people. To win freedom, we need

---

[22] *Mathrubhumi*, 21 August 1946. Kesava Menon's story is in *Kazhinja Kalam* (Calicut: Mathrubhumi Press, 1971).

all the people from Kashmir to Kanyakumari and Peshawar to Manipur to join together. They are prepared for that. They will do it.

We said this, which is the 'mistake' we committed. We haven't made any other mistakes. We also desire that the struggle must not be diverted into communalism. We are also concerned about the communal riots in Calcutta.

If *Mathrubhumi*'s concern about communal riots is genuine, then they have to promote the mentality of struggle amongst the workers and peasants and the people in the princely states. Why? Because the only remedy to the communal disturbances is the united struggle of the people of all communities against the British, the Kings in the princely states, the landlords, and the capitalists.

Mathrubhumi should also oppose the anti-Muslim speeches of Congress leaders in the same way as they oppose the communal speeches of the Muslim League.

Otherwise, if *Mathrubhumi* desire that any revolt — even the revolution against the British regime — should not rise up, then it would be good if they say so openly.[23]

EMS wrote a comprehensive essay on the revolt, which draws from his 1943 booklet on the history of peasant struggles in Kerala. We have selected this essay for this volume, since it provides, as many have pointed out, a considered assessment of the rebellion and one that has significantly shaped subsequent scholarly work.[24]

Based on EMS's intervention, we understand that the conflict in Malabar emerged from the objective conditions of the agrarian

---

[23] E.M.S. Namboodiripad, 'Does *Mathrubhumi* oppose a communal riot or mass struggle?', *Deshabhimani*, 22 August 1946.

[24] Two key books we have used in this introduction: Conrad Wood, *The Moplah Rebellion and Its Genesis*, New Delhi: People's Publishing House, 1987 and *Against Lord and State: Religion and Peasant Uprisings in Malabar, 1836-1921*, New Delhi: Oxford University Press, 1989.

crisis, but it manifests itself in the subjective appearance of Malabar's social history. The Moplah uprising was *not* a religious uprising, but it appeared as such to the eyes of some people due to the factors EMS proposed in a provisional manner and for further exploration. In addition, no analysis should neglect the historical evidence that the colonial State used agent provocateurs to *create* communal events as part of its propaganda effort.

After independence, the legislators in the Madras Assembly took up a discussion of the Malabar Tenancy (Amendment) Bill of 1953. At that time, Malabar district was part of Madras (the state of Kerala was formed in 1956). In the Assembly, the debate returned to the 1921 rebellion. The main protagonists in the debate were P. Ramamurthi, the Communist leader, and C. Rajagopalachari, the Congress leader who was the Chief Minister of Madras state. The debate reveals the fissures between the Communist interpretation of the revolt and the bourgeois-communal interpretation of the revolt:[25]

P. RAMAMURTHI: Sir, now I would like to speak on the Bill that is now before the House. This is a very important Bill in spite of the fact that it touches only a part of the State, viz., Malabar district and I hope Members who have come here from other parts of the State will evince keen interest in this Bill and take the fullest share in its discussion and voting. The question of tenancy is nothing new to this house. It has been before the House for nearly thirty years. But I would like to go a little back to the days when this struggle started. The urgency of the problem was so great in Malabar a century ago, that there were several revolts, peasant revolts in that part of the State. In 1884, there was a peasant revolt. Again in 1921, there was staged one of the biggest of revolts which was otherwise called

---

[25] Debate on the Malabar Tenancy (Amendment) Bill, 1953 in the Madras Assembly, 6 January 1954, pp. 225-227.

the Moplah Rebellion. The British Government did not like the revolt to be called an agrarian revolt and tried to give it a communal turn.

C. RAJAGOPALACHARI: The hon. Member probably had not much knowledge of the details of the Moplah Rebellion. That was entirely over the Khilafat question and there was a rumour circulated that a Turkish ship was waiting in the harbour and hence the rebellion.

C. SUBRAMANIAM (Congress; Minister of Food, Finance, Elections): That is the Russian method of talking.

T. C. NARAYANAN NAMBIAR (CPI member from Taliparamba, Malabar): It is not so. The Kerala Provincial Congress Committee itself has passed a unanimous resolution stating that it was an agrarian revolt.

C. RAJAGOPALACHARI: The hon. Member is too young, I fear, to speak authoritatively on what happened in 1920. I was in it. I was in Malabar also and I lived with some of the prisoners for some time in prison also. The hon. Member is very wrong in connecting agrarian matters with this. There was no agrarian agitation. But of course, the Communists' technique is to make everything agrarian and industrial.

P. RAMAMURTHI: In spite of the remarks of the Hon. the Chief Minister that it was not connected with agrarian matters, I must beg to differ from him, and I would like to tell him that I do not accept his opinion as based on history nor do I accept him to be an authority on history.

C. RAJAGOPALACHARI: I was referring to my personal experience.

P. RAMAMURTHI: I admit that the Chief Minister was in jail with some of the Moplah prisoners. The fact that he was in that area at that particular time does not mean that he knows the entire history of the origin of the Moplah Rebellion. Therefore, I do not want to enter into a controversy over this fact.

C. RAJAGOPALACHARI: That I am not an authoritative historian will be admitted even by me. But when it comes from the Leader of the Opposition, he cannot put forward the claim that on the connected subjects he is an authority.

P. RAMAMURTHI: Neither do I claim to be an authority on this subject. What is relevant to our purpose now is this: We must consider the course and development of that so-called rebellion in which thousands of Malayalees belonging to each and every community went against the landlords. It all happened during the period of the rebellion and the Congress Committee itself has recorded this fact.

C. RAJAGOPALACHARI: I dispute its correctness.

P. RAMAMURTHI: The Hon. Chief Minister may dispute it but the organisation to which he belongs, viz., the Congress, has itself after a full enquiry come to the conclusion that the revolt was an agrarian revolt and that it had its origin in agrarian discontent. I take the Malabar Congress Committee to be a greater authority which has direct knowledge of the people and their condition than the Chief Minister.

C. RAJAGOPALACHARI: When was the resolution passed?

P. RAMAMURTHI: I think in the year 1929.

C. RAJAGOPALACHARI: The Rebellion took place in 1921 and the resolution was passed in 1929.

P. RAMAMURTHI: It was a resolution which went into the whole matter. It was passed after detailed enquiry into the history of the rebellion. So, I do not want to dilate on this question further. I would like to point out that this kind of organised agitation has been going on for a very long time. In 1930, therefore, the British Government thought it necessary for the first time to satisfy the peasants with some reform if they wanted to avoid rebellions for ever. Although they were able to suppress the earlier rebellion, they feared that many more might crop up unless they undertook some legislation to satisfy the demands of the peasants at least partially. And so, the 1930 Act came. But even then, the British Government did not want to do away with the rights of the landlord class because the Government wanted the support of the landlord element for their own existence. They did not want to touch their rights to any fundamental or material extent. Therefore, the agitation continued for some more years and the Congress Party itself, which was no opposition to the then Government, supported it. As a result of this opposition to the original Act, the Kuttikrishna Menon Committee came, and it submitted its report in 1940.

Ramamurthi never flinched. He stood firm against the attempt by the senior Congress leader to reduce the complexity of the Malabar Rebellion of 1921 to a communal affair.

INFLAMMATIONS OF HINDUTVA

When the Communists put forward a scientific assessment of the rebellion, the Hindutva forces offered a less scientific and more inflammatory story. The story that is now being promoted by the political forces of Hindutva is derived from the work of the key work of the Arya Samaj in 1921. Tagore's 1937 report revealed the role of the Arya Samaj in the creation of the Hindutva storyline regarding the Malabar revolt:

The Arya-Samajists who, under the protection of the government went to different centres of the rebellion, took photos of the very few Hindus who were killed by the Moplahs and triumphantly displayed the 'horror of Moplah atrocities' to the Hindus. Very significantly, they did nothing this time to collect materials about atrocities committed by the soldiers or to take snaps of hundreds of Moplah peasants shot and hanged and of Moplah women outraged and molested by the soldiers. The Arya Samajists till this day, exhibit these photos of those Hindus who, by the way, acted as spies and informers to the government which led to the arrest of hundreds of Moplah peasants. Communalism hiding under a humanitarian cloak is always mean and cowardly.

In 1921, the Punjab Arya Prathinidhi Sabha sent Pandit Rishi Ram, son of Arya Samaj President Mahatma Hans Raj, to Calicut on a mission.[26] Having heard rumours about forced conversion of Hindus to Islam, Pandit Rishi Ram arrived in Malabar to begin the process called *shuddhi* or re-conversion. The Arya Samaj gathered sporadic stories of violence against Hindus and circulated these widely amongst the aristocrats, the landlords, and the political forces of the Hindu Right. The Arya Samaj stories formed the basis for the book assembled by Diwan Bahadur C. Gopalan Nair, *The Moplah Rebellion, 1921*, published in 1923. Nair was the Deputy Collector of Malabar, and he dedicated his book to Captain P. McEnroy, who had led the forces to crush the rebellion. Nair's book sparkled with the kind of rumours and sporadic incidents that became facts in the Hindutva imagination. Appendix X of Nair's book lists atrocities, including mass conversions to Islam, burning and looting of Hindu and Christian homes, and desecrating and destroying temples.[27] Nair did not bother with evidence for these feverish claims, much of it derived from the organisations such as the Arya Samaj (including photographs that came to Nair directly from Pandit Rishi Raj). He inflamed their importance and suggested that they defined the totality of the rebellion.

B. S. Moonje, the leader of the Hindu Mahasabha, came to Calicut in 1923 to meet with the Zamorin and sections of the Brahmanical elite. He read Nair's book and absorbed the materials circulated by the Arya Samaj. Moonje brought the full apparatus of the Hindu Mahasabha to manufacture consent about stories

---

[26] Eliza Kent, "'Mass Movements' in South India, 1877-1936', *Converting Cultures. Religion, Ideology and Transformations of Modernity*, eds. Dennis Washburn and A. Kevin Reinhart, Leiden: Brill, 2007, p. 387.

[27] C. Gopalan Nair, *The Moplah Rebellion, 1921*, Calicut: Norman Printing Bureau, 1923, p. 52. Parts of this material would reappear in C. Sankaran Nair's *Gandhi and Anarchy*, Madras: Tagore Press, 1923, Appendix V.

of rape and forced conversion, stories that started as ill-founded rumours and then became dogma for members of the Hindu Right.[28]

False rumours of the rebellion as a communal riot reached the ears of V. D. Savarkar, who was then in prison in Ratnagiri. He had read C. Gopalan Nair's book. This book, written by a pro-British bureaucrat, inspired Savarkar to write an equally zealous political tract and bilious novel. The tract was *Hindutva: Who is a Hindu?* (1924), where Savarkar wrote, 'This one word, Hindutva, ran like a vital spinal cord through our whole body poetic and made the Nayars of Malabar weep over the sufferings of the Brahmins of Kashmir.'[29] The next year, Savarkar wrote a novel, *Moplah*, which told a sensational story of terror against Hindus. These books kept alive the spurious list from Appendix X of Nair's 1923 book. The Rashtriya Swayamsevak Sangh (RSS) founded in 1925, was built on these false stories of sexual violence and forced conversion in Malabar that had been circulated by the Arya Samaj, C. Gopalan Nair, Savarkar, and Moonje.

It is true that the scientific historical profession did not take seriously the work of Nair and Savarkar on the Malabar Rebellion. This was particularly so since they were devoid of evidence. But, in recent years, these older theories have made a comeback, with the Hindutva forces gaining political power. In 2021, the joint secretary of the Vishwa Hindu Parishad, G. Sthanumalayan, published a book to commemorate the 100th anniversary of the rebellion. The book is about the 'gruesome, macabre acts of the Moplah rebellion', writes Sthanumalayan.[30] On 19 August 2021, RSS supremo Ram Madhav said that the Malabar Rebellion was an

---

[28] Charu Gupta, *Sexuality, Obscenity, Community: Women, Muslims, and the Hindu Public in Colonial India*, New Delhi: Permanent Black, 2001, pp. 225-226.

[29] V. D. Savarkar, *Hindutva: Who is a Hindu?*, Bombay: Veer Savarkar Prakashan, 1969, p. 46.

[30] G. Stanumalayan, *Nootraandu Kaanum Maapla Kalavaram*, Chennai: Vijayabharatham Prasuram, 2021.

early indicator of the 'Taliban mindset' in India. An organisation affiliated with the RSS — Prajna Pravah — wants to use the term 'genocide' to define the uprising; they would like to erect a 'genocide memorial' in Malabar. This attitude is no longer marginal. In 2019, the Ministry of Culture (Government of India) and the Indian Council of Historical Research (ICHR) published volume 5 of the *Dictionary of Martyrs. India's Freedom Struggle, 1857-1947.* It contains 387 'Moplah martyrs', including many people mentioned in this collection. The ICHR is now under pressure to remove these names from the book. It would like to erase the struggle of the people of Malabar against British imperialism and the landlord class, the two political projects of imperialism and landlordism with which the Hindutva right has no quarrel.

THE PARIS COMMUNE OF MALABAR

In 1944, communists and others marched in southern Malabar to demand the demolition of the memorial to the District Superintendent of Police R. H. Hitchcock, who led the crushing of the Malabar Rebellion (Hitchcock wrote a confidential history of the rebellion in 1925 that laid the groundwork for further counter-insurgency operations by the colonial State).[31] The participants in the march sang a war song (*padappat*) as they approached the memorial to Hitchcock. The Communist poet Kambalath Govindan Nair wrote this war song, which opens the introduction:

Manjeri ninnanchaaru mailu
doorame mongaththilu
Sancharikkunnorkk
kaanaaraakumaa niraththilu
Chaththupoya Hitchcock
saayivinte smaarakam
Chaaththane kudivechcha pole

---

[31] R. H. Hitchcock, *The History of the Malabar Rebellion, 1921*, Madras: Government Press, 1926.

aa balaalil smaarakam
Nammalute nenchilaanaa
kallu naatti vechchath
Nammalute koottareyaanaa
suvaru konnath
raajyasneham veerukonda
dheerarundee naattilu
Raksha venamenkil
Mandikkottavar Englandilu

On the road to Mongam
Miles away from Majeri
You can see the dead Hitchcock's memorial.
The real satan's tomb.
That stone was laid on our chest.
That pig killed our brothers.
This land has brave patriots.
Oh, White Men!
If you want to live long,
escape to England soon.

They could not bring down the statue. It was later moved to Calicut. Nair lost his job. *Deshabhimani*, the Communist Party paper which published the *padappat*, was confiscated. The song was banned.

In 1939, A.K. Gopalan — AKG — went to work in the Eranad *taluk* to build the peasant movement there. His speeches about the exploitation of the peasants and the oppression of the Muslim peasantry specifically made an impact in the area. The peasants told him about the Malabar Rebellion, their role in that uprising, and in the brutality of the colonial State. Their attention was focused on the memorial to Hitchcock. They wanted to build a movement against the Hitchcock monument and recover their history.

A *jatha* had started out under the leadership of Appakoya and Yusuf with the object of removing Hitchcock's Memorial. It was called the Hitchcock Memorial Removal *Jatha*. I toured various parts of Eranad with this *jatha*, and was thus able to make the acquaintance of our Muslim brothers there. It was at this time that I was able to strengthen my ties with Abdul Rahiman, Moidu Moulvi, and others. My association with Abdul Rahiman helped to an extent in turning me into a seasoned agitator.[32]

This was the *jatha* that sang the *padappat*.

In 1946, AKG was elected to be the Secretary of the Communist Party of India in Kerala. Strikes of rail and postal workers shook the State. In his memoirs, he writes,

EMS wrote an article in *Deshabhimani* entitled 'Call and Warning'. I spoke accordingly in a meeting in Eranad. I was arrested while returning. EMS was arrested at the same time. We were released later on bail. Krishna Pillai was banished to Travancore.[33]

The arrest of EMS and AKG took place because of the political upsurge in India. But the proximate reason was their agitational work amongst the Moplahs about the Malabar Rebellion. That was what EMS had written about and that was the subject of AKG's speech. AKG delivered his speech at a public meeting in Perinthalmanna on 25 August 1946; he was held in prison till two weeks after India won its independence. In the speech, AKG related the 1921-22 rebellion to the struggles of Bhagat Singh and to the four Kayyur martyrs — Madathil Appu, Kunhambu Nair,

---

[32] A.K. Gopalan, *In the Cause of the People. Reminiscences*, New Delhi: Orient Longman, 1973, p. 90.

[33] A.K. Gopalan, *In the Cause of the People*, p. 163.

Chirukandan, Abu Baker — who had led a historic rural rebellion in 1939-41 under the banner of the Kisan Sabha. 'The good lessons of 1921 have to be learnt', he said, which were the importance of direct action, the necessity of courage and intelligence, and the perils of communal division ('Hindus and Muslims should not cut each other's throats', he warned). But the rising was only one-half of the lesson. AKG pointed out that the Moplah rebellion foreshadowed the Quit India movement of 1942, whose high point was the establishment in large parts of India, areas free of British Rule (such as the Patri Sarkar in Sangli district). The rebellion showed the importance of installing a 'government by the labourers and the peasants', the Paris Commune in Malabar, with Wariankunnath Kunhammad Haji, 'a poor cart man, a man who had not passed any examination' who was the 'leader of the poor' and who presided over a State in which no officials took bribes, communalism was set aside, and social welfare was the norm.

It is this memory of the Malabar Rebellion that the communists have kept alive, a history that we share with you in this little book.

The Moplah Rising, 1922

Abani Mukherji[1]

The Moplah rebellion of August and September last, and the more recent incident of the suffocation of a truck load of Moplah prisoners in a travelling 'Black hole of Calcutta' will be fresh in the memory of readers of the [Communist] Review. Comrade Mukherji's account of the troubles on the Malabar coast brings three points into relief:

1) *that the Moplah risings have always been primarily manifestations of the class war;*

2) *that the attempts (usually well meant) of the British authorities to improve the lot of the poor peasants have invariably resulted under capitalism in strengthening the position of the native capitalist class;*

3) *that the element of religious fanaticism which has always attended Moplah outbreaks, is receding into the background, and that a solidarity of Mohammedan and Hindu oppressed against their oppressors (Hindu or Mohammedan, European or Asiatic) is coming to the front. This last is what Lord Northcliffe, revisiting India, finds so alarming.*

One word more of introduction. It is interesting to read an honest British official's view of these matters. In 1881 Mr William Logan was appointed to enquire into the Moplah question. In his great work on Malabar, Logan gave a history of the Moplah risings

---

[1] *Communist Review*, vol. 2, no. 5, March 1922.

prior to that date, and an account of his mission of enquiry. He sums up the matter as follows (Malabar, Vol. 1, p.588, published 1887): 'Mr Logan finally formed the opinion that the Moplah outrages were designed to counteract the overwhelming influence, when backed by the British courts, of the Jenmis [landlords] in the exercise of their novel powers of ouster [eviction] and of rent-raising conferred upon them'. The phrase when 'backed by the British courts' is peculiarly significant!

CLEMENS PALME DUTT AND ELNA DUTT,
COMMUNIST REVIEW

On 19 August 1921, a rising began in Malabar, the southwestern province of the Madras presidency. According to current reports, number of Moplah peasants, incited by the nationalists of Khilafat movement, had taken up arms against the Government as by law established. Their aim was said to be the overthrow of British rule in India.

It was also asserted that the primary aim of these fanatical Mohammedans was to re-establish the independence of Turkey on its old footing. After the first skirmish, we were informed, the aims of the Khilafat movement had been forgotten, and the *mullahs*, the bigoted leaders, had directed the attack of the Mohammedan rank and file against their peaceful Hindu neighbours, who were being offered the alternative, 'Death or Islam'. The result had been the forcible conversion to Mohammedanism of the members of some eighty Hindu families, and the slaughter of a few dozen more who had preferred death to disgrace and the loss of religion.

In addition, we were told that the Moplah masses were well armed, not only with staves and with war-knives and swords improvised out of saws in the village smithies, but also with firearms secured by raids on police stations and upon the arsenal of the military depot of Malappuram, in the centre of Moplah territory. These facts were reported in order to show that the rising had been carefully planned by the leaders of the Khilafat movement, who for months had been preaching a boycott of the British throughout the country.

The details of the report are historically correct, but the fallacious inference is deliberately supplied by the Government whose interest is to mislead the population. The main object of the Government in spreading the false notion of the causes of the rising is to break up the newly acquired unity in the fighting forces of the inhabitants of India. And the Government policy was shrewd, for all the nationalist papers, and especially those published by Hindus, were agreed in condemning the Moplahs, and in demanding that the government should take such measures as would effectively prevent the recurrence of similar disasters.

Being personally acquainted with the Moplah country and the Moplah people, I was amazed to find that even *Pravda* [the newspaper of the Communist Party of the Soviet Union] had allowed itself to be fooled by these governmental lies. Data collected from available periodicals, in conjunction with the current reports received during recent months from the areas affected by the present rising, show clearly that it was, in the first instance, a peasant revolt directed against landlords and moneylenders. One point which should suffice to show that religious fanaticism was not the primary cause of the trouble is that the first victim of the insurgents was Khan Bahadur K. V. Chekutty, a retired police inspector, landowner, and moneylender — a Mohammedan. Moreover, the Moplahs were just as fiercely incensed against Moplah landlords as against Hindu landlords, although the former belonged to their race and religion.

We must also bear in mind that the insurgents had a special interest in burning the offices where the Governmental registers and the family archives of the native magnates (capitalists and landowners) were kept, thus destroying the legal evidence of mortgages and other debts of the peasant population. The first action taken by Moplah Swaraj (Home Rule Organisation) was to issue a proclamation for the remission of taxation. The Moplah rising was but a continuance of the peasant disturbances which during recent years have occurred in various parts of India. In 1920, there was a peasant uprising in Oudh (Northern India), when the insurgents adopted a similar tactic to those of the Moplahs and burned the houses of the wealthier natives. The main distinction between the Oudh rising and the Malabar rising is that the Oudh peasants were better organised. They had established a definite union known as Kisan Sabhas (Peasants Union).

The word Moplah is derived from the Tamil word *mupala* which means son-in-law. The story runs that long ago an Arab friend of a local chief, having married a girl who was one of the latter's kin, became known as 'the son-in-law', and that subsequently all the Arabs settlers received the same name. At any rate, the Moplahs are the offspring of Arab warriors, who established themselves on the Malabar coast nearly one thousand years ago, but, of course, their Arab blood has become greatly mixed. There are about one million of them in all. They can be readily distinguished from the other Moslems of the region by their tall, slender, and well-built frames, and by their high-spirited, not to say, quarrelsome disposition. Moplahs are found in considerable numbers in only five of the thirteen taluks or districts of the Malabar coast, namely, in Valluvanad, Ponnani, Eranad, Calicut, and Wayanad. The chief town of Malabar is Calicut, the well-known seaport at which Vasco da Gama first landed in India in the year 1498. This is the leading commercial centre of the region.

In this part of India, social oppression is more extreme than elsewhere, and the terrible tyranny of the caste system is more conspicuous; for these reasons Christianity has made more headway here than in other regions of Hindustan. It is worth noting that among the Nair Hindus of Malabar, a modified form of matriarchy still prevails. The area is predominantly agricultural, so that most of the population is directly dependent upon the soil for a livelihood. The members of what are termed the higher castes, those which have social precedence, are likewise the owners of the land. They thus exercise simultaneously a social and economic domination over the poorer classes. There has been in Malabar an active movement against the injustices from which the poorer members of the population suffer; but, owing to the economic dependence of the latter, the victims of social tyranny have not been able to achieve any notable improvement in their condition. 'After years of unhappy experiences, the masses have become convinced that the social emancipation is impossible to secure in the absence of economic enfranchisement', writes *Justice*, an anti-Brahmin daily newspaper of Madras.

The land in Malabar is in the actual possession of a class of persons known as Jenmis. They pay the Government a rent, the amount being arbitrarily fixed by the local authorities every ten years. Some of the Jenmis are Hindus and others are Mohammedans; but they all belong to the upper class. They sublet the land in smaller lots to the cultivators. In most cases, indeed, there are several stages in the subletting process, so that by the time we reach the peasant who tills the soil, three or four different persons have acquired an interest in the produce of his holding. Of course, by this disastrous system the amount payable in rent is continually enhanced, until at length the total falls with a crushing weight upon the head of the unlucky peasant.

The tiller of the soil has to devote most of his energies to paying these charges upon the land, so that there is but a narrow barrier between him and the famine.

Besides the Jenmis, we have to consider another factor in the life of Malabar peasants. I refer to the Kanomdars or money lenders, whose power over the land is obtained by making loans at usurious interest (ranging from 100 per cent to 700 per cent), either to the Jenmis or directly to the peasants. In some cases, the Kanomdars buy from the Jenmis the right of subletting the land and the right thus acquired is known as the Kanom-leasehold-right. The Kanomdars, to whom the landlord rights are transferred in this fashion, are nothing more than moneylenders. They are not peasant farmers at all. 'To speak of them as "farmers" is quite erroneous; it is only through the power of money that they hold sway over the land', writes *The Hindu* of Madras, a nationalist daily paper. The Kanomdars began to emerge as a class about a century ago, at a time when wealth was accumulating at the hands of the intellectuals, the forerunners of bourgeois of India. These intellectuals who are numerous in themselves, though they form so small a proportion of the population, make money as officials, lawyers, doctors, traders, etc., and like to invest their savings in land. Indeed, since manufacturing industry is still comparatively underdeveloped and is hampered in various ways, and since the interest on the Government loan is too low to be attractive, the land is practically the only field of investment. Such persons have become Kanomdars. They are eager to increase their capital by fair means or foul, and they try to squeeze the uttermost farthing out of the unhappy peasants.

It is obvious that Kanomdars, as a superfluous and unproductive class, must exercise a disastrous influence upon the agrarian system of Malabar. In fact, they have helped to promote the economic ruin of the country.

Thanks to this abominable agrarian system, peasant revolts have been a frequent occurrence in Malabar. For the last seventy years, the Government has found it necessary to maintain a European garrison at Malappuram, and the first important rising occurred in the year 1836. This led to the passing of an agrarian law which was to protect the peasantry from extortion. In 1854, after another rising, the Moplah War Knives Act was promulgated, forbidding the Moplahs to manufacture or own the long war-knives, which were almost the only weapons obtainable. But in 1887 came yet another and very serious rising, when thousands of Moplahs were shot down. The insurgents had refused to surrender, feeling that the only choice open to them was death by the bullet and death by slow starvation. The slaughter was followed by Governmental enquiry, and subsequently a new law was promulgated, the Tenant Right Act, which was intended to protect the tillers of the soil. None of these measures had any practical effort towards improving the situation of the exploited peasants, for the interpretation of the letter of the law was almost entirely in the hands of the lesser officials — natives personally interested in the system of extortion. Thus, the legislation was farcical. In 1900, when there had been further disturbances, another law was passed, the Farming Improvement Act. This did not pretend to give the peasant any economic security, but merely to safeguard him against eviction.

We have to remember that Malabar is almost exclusively an agricultural country, and that nearly all the population makes its living out of the soil. Ninety-nine per cent of the Moplahs are poor peasants. The law of 1900 was advantageous to Kanomdars and in a lesser degree to the sub-lessees. It did absolutely nothing to improve the lot of the working peasants.

The peasant troubles arose out of the fact that the Kanomdars were specially favoured by the Farming Improvement Act of 1900 and were planning to make themselves the sole lords of the soil. For this purpose, a meeting of Kanomdars was held on 18 July 1921, in the Valluvanad district of Malabar, a district largely peopled by Moplahs. The meeting took place at Tutakal, in the residence of N. P. Ahmed Kutti, a wealthy timber merchant, a Mohammedan. Eight hundred Kanomdars were present, both Hindus and Mohammedans. The chair was taken by a Hindu, K. Koru Nair, a noted lawyer of Ottapalam. A resolution was passed to petition the Government for a law to confirm the Kanom-farmers (!) of Malabar in their possession. Bahadur M. K. Nair, a Hindu, retired Government official, Kanon-farmer and moneylender, member of the legislative council of Madras, was appointed to push the matter of the 'Tenancy Bill' in Government circles. We must carefully note that whenever such persons use the term 'farmer' and have it employed in legislative enactments they are referring to Kanom-farmers and not to the poor peasants. It is the contention of the

Kanomdars that the legislation they propose is the only way by which the agrarian difficulties of Malabar can be overcome. The resolution adopted at this meeting was duly brought before the legislative council of Madras and was favourably received by the Government notwithstanding the vigorous opposition of the Jenmis and the more enlightened among the peasants. Although the law had not yet been put in force, the Kanomdars confident of their coming success had begun to exercise the expected rights, so that the patience of the oppressed peasants was at length exhausted. The outcome was the Moplah rising of 19 August, which has now become a matter of history.

The non-political character of the rising can be read between the lines of the report of a speech made by Lord Reading, the Viceroy, to a joint meeting of the Council of the State and the Indian Legislative Assembly. I quote from *The Times* of 6 September 1921:

The spark which kindled the flame was the resistance by a large and hostile crowd of Moplahs, armed with swords and knives, to a lawful attempt by the police to affect certain arrests in connection with a case of housebreaking. The police were powerless to effect the capture of the criminals, and the significance of the incident is that it was regarded as a defeat of the police, and therefore of the Government.

The actual facts were as follows: Since the hot-headed Moplahs had no other resource against the oppression practiced on them by the Kanomdars and the Jenmis, they took the law into their own hands and burned some of the oppressors' houses at Tiruzangadi, a town in Eranad district. When the authorities set the police in motion and mobilised a company of Leinster regiment, (the British troops stationed at Malappuram) to arrest the ringleaders, a mob of two thousand persons resisted the police and the soldiers, who were forced to withdraw. Certain fanatical mullahs, such as Ali Musalier, Kunki Tangal, etc., seized the opportunity, with the aid of a few brigands, to raise the standard of the Khilafat movement for the overthrow of the Government.

These adventurers were in a favourable position to begin with, for they were able to seize firearms and ammunition from the recently evacuated police stations and military outposts of Eranad district, so that the British forces had to retreat. Moreover, the insurgents got possession of a sum equivalent to £40,000 from the strong box at Malappuram.

While affairs were taking this course in the towns, the coolies on the outlying plantations jumped at the chance of retaliating for the grievances they had suffered at the hands of the European planters, and they killed a planter named Eaton. 'The Englishman had time to fire only three shots from his revolver before being kicked to death by his own coolies'. Another planter, Tippets by name, 'would have been killed but for the loyalty of his servants, who said, 'We have been with the Sahib for five years and can any coolie present point out one act of injustice on the Sahib's part?' (*The Times*, 5 September 1921).

The nationalists and the leaders of the Khilafat movement declared Swaraj (Home Rule) and hoisted the green flag [the religious emblem of the Mohammedans — *Communist Review*], but the leaders were not able to prevent their followers from engaging in rapine and seeking immediate gain. Another official bulletin throws further light on the agrarian character of the movement:

A local Moplah landowner, his son, and their retainers, numbering over 100, had a miraculous escape. A rescue party found them in the jungle, hiding from the rebels, who had already declared Swaraj (Home Rule) and published a proclamation remitting taxation (*The Times*, 5 September 1921).

The Hindus suffered most from the wrath of the insurgents,

not because they were of a different religion from these, but because most of the oppressors are Hindus. In the interest of the bourgeois, the Moplahs have been shot down by machine guns, but the Government has not succeeded in suppressing by this slaughter the revolutionary sentiments of the poor peasants and workmen of India.

Peasants Revolt in Malabar, 1921

Saumyendranath Tagore[1]

The first quarter of the twentieth century was coming to a close. The world-war had shaken the foundation of world-Imperialism. India was seething with discontent. The success of the revolution in Russia, had opened up a new horizon before the oppressed of the entire world. The non-cooperation movement had been started with great promise, only to be abandoned at the crucial moment by its leader. Spontaneous movements of the masses raised their heads from all corners of this vast land.

The revolt of the peasants in Malabar, in 1921, constitutes, so far as India is concerned, the greatest manifestation of spontaneous mass upheaval in the first quarter of this century, against British Imperialism.

After the revolt had been suppressed, the government published a report of the uprising, in three volumes. But the Government withheld its own publication from the public, confining its circulation only amongst the officials.

Apart from this Government report, no other authentic account of this peasant uprising has yet been published. This brochure is a meagre attempt to record the causes and the principal events of the uprising. Future historians, while dealing with the freedom's movement in India, will, I am sure, do the fullest justice to this heroic struggle of the peasantry against feudalism supported by

[1] Bombay: T. Godiwala, 1937.

Imperialism. It represents one of the most poignant chapters of spontaneous mass-uprising in India.

Malabar, the ancient land of Kerala, is situated on the Western seacoast of Southern India. It covers an area of five thousand seven hundred and ninety-two square miles and is one of the most fertile and beautiful regions of India.

In the year 1922, according to the census report, the population of Malabar numbered 30,98,871, that is to say, it was little over three millions. In 1922, the Eranad district which played such an important role in the agrarian uprising, had a population of four hundred thousands, of which 1,63,328 were Hindus and 2,36,612 were Muslims.

The Muslims of Malabar are called Moplahs. They are mostly poor peasants and the Moplahs of the Eranad district are no exception to this rule. Only those Moplahs who are engaged in the timber trade on the coast of the river Chaliar, and their number is small compared to the entire Moplah population, could be said to be slightly better off than the rest. In the hilly tracts of Nilambur and Wandoor also, there are a few well-to-do Moplahs who cultivate lands taken on lease from the Government. Very few amongst the Moplahs are landlords.

The chief occupation of the Moplahs is agriculture. The Moplah peasants are very hard-working; they reclaim the forestlands, which lie uncultivated for ages, only to be ejected from the reclaimed lands by the landlords, who usurp them for their own use. The Moplah peasants are either leaseholders or are mere wage-labourers who earn their living, cultivating other peoples' land. Quite a large number of Moplahs work in the bamboo forests in the eastern mountain-regions and since a decade or two, quite a large number of Moplahs work in the rubber plantations.

In Malabar, the landlords are almost all Hindus and are moreover mostly Brahmins; only in the North Malabar there are a few Moplah landlords. Oppressed and exploited as the Moplah peasants are, they harbour in their minds, since ages, a bitter hatred against their oppressors, the landlords.

Previous to the great peasant revolt of 1921, there were about fifty Moplah peasant uprisings in Malabar. In seventeen years, between 1836 to 1853, there were no less than twenty-two peasant uprisings. Only in a few cases, the apparent causes of these riots were religious. At times, some trouble regarding the site of the Mosque or regarding conversion from one religion to the other led to bloodshed, but in most cases as we shall see from the accounts given below, the causes of the uprisings were purely agrarian.

Centuries ago, the Arab traders from Arabia came to India, and some of them had settled down in the Southern coast of Malabar. The Moplahs are the descendants of these Arab dealers and the Hindu Nair women. It was Para Nambi, the commander-in-chief of the Raja of Calicut, who allowed the Moplahs for the first time to settle down in the Eranad district and to erect mosques. Malappuram was the headquarters of Para Nambi. In the early years of the Nineteenth Century, as a result of a dispute between Para Nambi and the Moplahs regarding the mosque, Para Nambi wanted to demolish the mosques. Fierce fight took place between the troops of Nambi and the Moplahs, as a result of which forty-seven Moplahs were killed.

The uprising of 1841 was against one Terumpalli Namboodiri, a landlord who took away by force the leasehold plots of land of the Moplah peasants. The leader of the uprising was one Kunjolan, himself a Moplah peasant. The landlord was killed, and his house burnt down. The military force hastened to the rescue of the landlord and shot down scores of peasants.

In the uprising of 1843, the Moplah peasants killed one Kaprat Krishna Panikkar who was the headman of the village Thurangadi. In the same year, during another uprising, the Moplah peasants murdered one Karukamanna Moose, a Brahmin landlord. In the year 1851, a peasant uprising raised its head in Kottayam Taluk of

North Malabar. A group of Moplah peasants besieged the house of Kalathil Kesavan Thangal, a landlord, and massacred his entire family. In 1880, a band of Moplah peasants attacked Appadurai Pattar and Krishna Pisharodi, both [upper-caste] landlords. The peasants were shot dead by the armed guards of the landlords.

In those days Lord Buckingham was the governor of Madras. He received an anonymous letter in which the miserable conditions of the Moplah peasants were described in detail. The letter pointed out the many grievances of the Moplah peasants and the cruel exploitation to which the Moplah peasants were subjected to by the landed aristocracy. The writer or writers of that letter requested the Governor to pass orders suspending all litigations filed against the Moplah peasants by the landlords. The Governor was also warned that if he did not take these steps as suggested by the letter, a serious uprising of the Moplah peasants was inevitable. Lord Buckingham took immediate steps. A committee of enquiry was formed with the District Judge and the Collector of Malabar to enquire into the grievances of the peasantry. In their report both the officials admitted that the tenancy problem was at the root of the trouble. Another committee was set up to make a detailed enquiry into the existing tenancy system, the practice of ejectment of the tenants and the vicious system of arbitrary demand for payment by the landlords for the improvements of plots which the tenants had improved by hard labour. Mr Logan reported in detail to the Government regarding the tenancy system and its abuses. As a result of this report the Malabar Tenancy Act (Malabar Kuzhikkoor Act) was passed in 1887.

In 1898, there was another uprising in which a landlord was killed by the Moplah peasants. It was in February 1919 that the last peasant uprising, prior to the great Moplah rebellion, took place. The uprising took place in a village called Mankatta Pallipuram, the estate of a Brahmin landlord. Chekaji, a Moplah peasant, having failed to pay the rents due to the landlord, was sued by the landlord who in due course secured a decree against him. Not being satisfied with this, the landlord went to the length of putting a stop to the marriage of Chekaji's son, which was settled. Chekaji with a group of Moplah peasants attacked the landlord and his men and killed them. They in their turn, were shot and killed by the soldiers.

What does this brief account of the most important Moplah uprisings prove? It proves beyond doubt that the oppression of the peasants by the landlords, the unjust tenancy laws, the numerous extortions of illegal dues which the landlords forcibly collected from the peasants, were the causes of these uprisings. Later on, religious fanaticism got mixed up with the main economic factors and the communal people on both sides, being encouraged by the third party, distorted and misrepresented these agrarian uprisings as communal ones. But as we have already noticed, even the enquiry committees set up by the Government were forced to admit that the tenancy system and the tyranny of the landlords, were the real causes of these peasant uprisings.

The great peasant revolt of 1921 came as the culmination of these numerous sporadic peasant uprisings throughout Malabar and had burst out again and again, for half a century. A tenancy movement was started in Calicut and the surrounding districts in October 1920. The main grievances of the peasantry which gave rise to this tenancy movement, were the increment of rent and the ejectments of the peasants from their holdings by the landlords. This movement was started quite independently of the Congress movement. One of its leaders, Narayan Menon joined the Congress only after he had severed all connections with the tenancy movement. The tenancy movement created a great stir in South Malabar. Thousands of peasants voiced in hundreds of meetings their demand for a more equitable tenancy system than the existing one and the total suppression of the unjust extortions by the landlords. The peasants advocated the boycott of the landlords and also of those persons who sided with the landlords. In numerous meetings the peasants took the vow that if a landlord ejects a peasant from his land, none will take that plot of ground on lease. Moreover, they would boycott the peasant who would take that land on lease, and they will not pay rents to the landlords. In some places the peasants boycotted the landlords socially.

The political atmosphere of South Malabar grew electric. The great peasant masses were stirred to their deepest depths. With each passing day their demands became more and more insistent and the intensity of the revolutionary fervour of the peasantry became more and more evident. At the peasants' Conference held at Manjeri in 1920 resolutions were passed supporting the demands of the peasantry. Peasant unions were organised at several places in Malabar. A Tenant Relief Association was organised in the feudal estate of the Raja of Calicut when a peasant was thrown out of the estate and a general strike was the result. None went to work in the landlords' field, none went to reap and gather his harvest. In different parts of the country the peasants refused to work for the landlords. Naturally British Imperialism could not suffer to see the landlord-class, its partner in exploitation of the Indian peasantry and one of its chief allies against Revolution in India, in grave danger, and not give it assistance. British Imperialism had to help the landlords for its own sake. Mr Thomas, the then Collector of Malabar, promulgated section 144 with the idea of throttling the newly formed peasant unions. This high-handedness on the part of the Government, instead of frightening the peasants, had just the contrary effect on them. It made them more resolute in their fight against the landlords. In the meantime, orders restricting the freedom of speeches and of holding meetings were passed by the Government against U. Gopala Menon, Wariankunnath Kunhammad Haji, and other leaders of the Tenancy movement.

In Malabar the Khilafat movement came into existence at this time when the Tenancy agitation was at its height. The first Khilafat meeting was held at Manjeri in 1920. In order to win over the Moplah peasantry which formed more than three-fourths of the Muslim population of Malabar; the Khilafat movement in

Malabar was forced to lend its support to the Tenancy movement. The leaders of both the movements, the Khilafat movement and the Tenancy movement, worked hand in hand and series of meetings were organised in Eranad and Valluvanad districts and also at Calicut, Tirurangadi, Kondolti, Manjeri, Malapuram, and other places.

On the 5 February 1921, the District Magistrate of South Malabar, promulgated section 144 prohibiting the peasant organisations to hold meetings. The text of the order of the District Magistrate is worth quoting. It runs thus:

The District Magistrate has received information that it has been decided to hold a series of Khilafat meetings in the Eranad district and that by holding such meetings there is an immediate danger that the feelings of the ignorant Moplahs will be inflamed against not only the Government but also against the Hindu Jenmies [landlords] of the district.

The district Magistrate who was there to safeguard the interest of the landlords, promulgated section 144 in Eranad and in a number of other districts of Malabar where the peasant unions were formed. Tenancy meetings were forcibly dispersed by the police. At Tirur, the policemen handled the peasants who assembled in a meeting in a dastardly manner. At Kalpakancheri, nearly twenty thousand men were present at a meeting where the police did all that lay in their power to provoke the people to violence. In a meeting held at Ponani the police started beating the people severely. Here the peasant masses retaliated, and the police took to their heels. The police violence did not intimidate the peasantry to submission. On the contrary, the peasants quickly realising the futility and ineffectiveness of passive resistance as a tactic of struggle began to prepare themselves for an armed rising.

On 18 August 1921, orders were passed for the arrest of M. P. Narayana Menon, Mammad Moosa, K. Abdullah Hazi of Pookkottur, and four others who were connected with the Tenancy and the Khilafat movements. Thomas, the district magistrate of Malabar, himself proceeded to Tirungadi with Police Superintendent Hitchcock, the Deputy Police Superintendent, and a batch of hundred soldiers and special police force. On the night of 19 August, the District Magistrate reached Tirungadi with his party. A second batch of Police and Military force came from Malapuram and joined Thomas and his party. On the morning of 20 August 1921, Thomas besieged and raided the mosque of Tirungadi, with the hope of arresting the men against whom warrants of arrest had been issued. Ali Mussaliar, the peasant leader was not found. The news of the raid spread like wildfire in the countryside and nearly thirty thousand Moplah peasants armed with all sorts of the weapons, came to defend their leaders. A fierce fight ensued. The police opened fire, killing nine men, and wounding many more; they arrested forty-one persons. A second batch of peasants attacked the police. The police, being hard-pressed took refuge in the court-building. Austin, the Collector, Rowley, the Assistant Superintendent of Police, one military officer and two constables were killed, by the peasants. Amongst the men whom the Police arrested, was Kunikhader, the secretary of the Malabar Khilafat Committee, who was hanged afterwards.

On 21 August, Tottenham, the Superintendent of Police of North Malabar, came to Parapangadi, a small place some two to three miles from Tirunangadi. He found that the railway lines between Parapangadi and Shoranur were removed, the railway stations were destroyed, telegraph wires had been cut off, and the bridges were destroyed. Post offices, Courts, Registration offices were plundered and burnt down. A handful of Government servants were molested and killed, and supporters of the Government were warned. Rebellion spread from Tirurangadi to Tirur, Parapangadi, Manjeri, Malapuram, Nilambur, Angadipuram, and Cherpulacheri. One of the first acts of the peasant-rebels was to proceed to Nilambur on 21 August, and plunder the house of the Raja of Nilambur, the wealthiest landlord of Eranad and the Valluvanad districts. The impoverished peasants took away corn and money. For a period of ten days the peasant rebels reigned supreme in that area; there was no trace of the military or police during those days.

Though during the rebellion and after it, the interested parties backed up by the third party, spread no pains to represent this peasant rebellion as a communal uprising of the Muslims against the Hindus none could dispute the fact that not a single Hindu was molested or plundered in those days just because he happened to be a Hindu. Some Hindus were killed by the rebels, but they were not killed because of their being Hindus; they were killed either because they supported the landlords or the Government. Only for this reason, the hirelings of the Raja of Nilambur who opposed the rebels and two supporters of the Government, one a munsif, and the other a retired Inspector of police, were killed by the Moplahs.

Narayana Menon, who was one of the leaders of the Tenancy movement and only later on had joined the non-co-operation movement as a convert to Gandhism, frankly admitted that the Moplah rebels never attacked the Hindus or robbed them out of communal considerations. When stray cases of looting were brought to the notice of the rebel-leaders, they severely punished the men responsible for looting the Hindu houses; sometime the punishment amounted to cutting off the hands of such offenders and the plundered things were immediately returned to the owners.

The Moplah peasant-rebels were not anti-Hindu by any means. They were violently anti-landlord and anti-government. Only when the Hindus allied themselves with the police and started giving information to the police about the whereabouts of the rebels who were hiding, that the Moplah peasant-rebels began looting Hindu-houses. Even then the Hindus who were known to be anti-government were not molested at all. In quite a number of places, the poor Hindu-peasants joined the Moplah rebels. Kunna Ahmad Hazi, a famous rebel peasant leader sent a letter to the *Hindu*, the well-known daily of Madras, in which he accused the Government of organising attacks on Hindu houses and temples and declared that the Moplah peasants had nothing to do with these attacks on the Hindus.

The landlords in a body supported the government against the peasants. Pumullimana, the richest landlord of Malabar, Pazi Yottumana, Kudallurmana, Chevurmana, Urupulasherimana, and the Raja of Nilambur, all these big landlords of Malabar sided entirely with the Government against the peasant-rebels. The same with the rich Moplahs; not only did they not join in the uprising, they actually opposed it and helped the government whole-heartedly.

Yogakshemam, the organ of the Malabar Brahmin, wrote in its leader of 6 January 1922, — 'Only the rich and the landlords are suffering at the hands of the rebels, not the poor peasants'.

One of the very first things that the rebels did at Manjeri, one of the chief centres of the rebellion, was to loot the bank, take all the ornaments that the poor people had mortgaged there, and return the ornaments to them.

Martial law was declared in Malabar on 21 August 1921. On 26 August, 75 British soldiers and 30 reserved police were engaged in a fight against ten thousand peasants at a place called Pookottur. Five hundred peasants were killed. On the government side, eight persons were killed and nine were seriously wounded. Guerrilla fight continued between the forces of the government and the rebels at various places. On 15 October 1921, there was severe fighting between the peasants and the government forces, at Vettikatturi, near Nilambur. Wariankunnath Kunhammad Haji, the famous peasant leader led the fight. Fourteen rebels were killed. From Burma, the government brought the Chinkan Chin regiment which reached Malapuram on 15 October; next day on 16 October, the Gurkha regiment arrived at Tirur. On 4 November

1921, Ali Mussaliar, one of the rebel-leaders and thirty others were tried and sentenced. Thirteen of them were sentenced to death, fifteen were sent to Andamans, only three were released on the ground of their being very young. On 13 November, fifty-six peasants were killed in a fight; on 14 of the same month, hundred and four were killed, and fourteen were taken prisoners. Twenty-five rifles were seized, and two soldiers were killed in a fight at Pondicat, a tiny place situated some ten miles from Nilambur. At Tamarasheri, the 28th Gurkha regiment was attacked by two thousand peasants. Fifty-eight rebels rushed into the camps of the Gurkha soldiers and were killed. Two hundred and fifty peasants were killed during this fight, and one was taken captive.

Towards the end of November, the rebellion was crushed. The resistance of the peasants to the tyranny of the landlords and the government broke down before the immensely superior armed forces of the government. On the 28 November 1921, hundred and twenty-seven Moplah prisoners were removed from Tirur to Bellari by train. The closed van in which these peasant-rebels were thrust in, measured eighteen feet in length and nine feet in width. When the train arrived at Bellari, it was found that fifty-six of the prisoners had died through suffocation and heat.

The Martial law summary court, which was established on 3 October l921, tried roughly 2830 peasant-rebels of whom 807 were committed to the sessions. In the jail of Coimbatore alone, two hundred rebels were hanged.

The atrocities perpetrated by the soldiers on the unarmed and defenceless men and women left behind in the Moplah villages, were appalling. Women were insulted and outraged, and houses were looted and burnt, and men were mercilessly belaboured. The rebels generally retired into the deep forest at the news of the approaching army. Mostly women were left behind in the villages and they were outraged and even murdered by the soldiers. In one particular case an old woman was assaulted and shot. Concentration camps were established where the Moplah women were gathered and held as hostages by the military. It must be said in fairness that the charges of brutality were brought only against the Chinkan Chin forces brought from Burma but never against the British Regiment. To strike terror in the hearts of the peasant masses, peasant-rebels were hanged on the wayside trees and left dangling there in order to create an 'impression' on the populace. Brutal terror was let loose on the peasantry by the military and the police.

The Arya-Samajists who, under the protection of the government went to different centres of the rebellion, took photos of the very few Hindus who were killed by the Moplahs and triumphantly displayed the 'horror of Moplah atrocities' to the Hindus. Very significantly, they did nothing this time to collect materials about atrocities committed by the soldiers or to take snaps of hundreds of Moplah peasants shot and hanged and of Moplah women outraged and molested by the soldiers. The Arya Samajists till this day, exhibit these photos of those Hindus who, by the way, acted as spies and informers to the government which led to the arrest of hundreds of Moplah peasants. Communalism hiding under a humanitarian cloak is always mean and cowardly.

As this peasants' rebellion broke out at a period, when the entire country was in a political ferment due to Mr Gandhi's non-co-operation movement, one can very pertinently enquire as to what was the attitude of Mr Gandhi and the Congress towards this peasants' uprising.

One Mr Yakub Hassan wrote a letter to Mr Gandhi, in which he dwelt at length on the misery of the Moplah peasants and the indescribable terror to which they have been subjected by the Martial law regime. He writes: 'Most of them (i. e. Moplahs) were cultivating lands under the petty landlords who are almost all Hindus. The oppression of the Jenmies (landlords) is a matter of notoriety and a long-standing grievance of the Moplahs that has never been redressed'. Further, dwelling on the subject of the forcible conversion of the Hindus to Islam, Mr Hassan observes,

'The Hindus have had their vengeance through the military who burnt the Moplah houses and their mosques wholesale. Thousands of Moplahs have been killed, shot, hanged, or imprisoned for life and thousands are now languishing in jail. Unfortunate circumstances, the causes of which I need not enter into on this occasion, forced him into the position of a rebel. He has done what anyone, Hindu, Muslim, or Christian under the same circumstances and in the same emergency would have done in self-defence and self-interest'.

As I have already pointed out, this peasants' rebellion furnishes us with a brilliant illustration of the fact how religion is introduced into issues, purely economic, by interested parties. Yakub Hassan has not been very analytical. If he were, he would not have said, 'The Hindus have had their vengeance', he would have remarked that the landlords who, in this particular case were Hindus, have had their vengeance on the Moplah peasants for having revolted against the tyranny of the landlords. The 'Unfortunate circumstances, the causes of which', Yakub Hassan unfortunately did not dwell upon in his letter to Mr Gandhi, are nothing but the most inhuman exploitation of these Moplah peasants carried on by the Jenmies (Landlords) of Malabar with the support of the government. Yakub Hassan has very rightly remarked that the Moplah peasant 'has done what anyone, Hindu, Muslim, or Christian, under the same circumstances and in the same emergency would have done in self-defence and self-interest'.

Commenting on this letter of Yakub Hassan, Mr Gandhi wrote an article 'The Starving Moplah', in his *Young India*. As is the usual practice with Mr Gandhi, in this article, he has completely missed or ignored the economic causes that led to this peasant rebellion and has ascribed this uprising entirely to religious causes. He writes, 'I know that the Hindus feel sore over what the Moplahs in 1921, did to their Hindu neighbour in Malabar'. Mr Gandhi took exception to Yakub Hassan's statement, 'he has done what anyone, Hindu, Muslim, or Christian, would have done' and wrote, 'No circumstances and no provocation however grave, could possibly justify forcible conversion'.

In a second article, 'The meaning of the Moplah rising,' written on 20 October 1921, Mr Gandhi wrote the following, 'The Moplah revolt is a test for Hindus and Musalmans. Can Hindu friendship survive the strain put upon it? Can Musalmans in the deepest recess of their hearts approve the conduct of the Moplahs? . . . The Hindus must have the courage and the faith to feel that they can protect their religion in spite of such fanatical eruptions. A verbal disapproval by the Musalmans of Moplah madness is no test of Musalman friendship. The Musalmans must naturally feel the shame and humiliation of the Moplah conduct about forcible conversion and looting'.

This is how Mr Gandhi analysed the causes of the peasants' revolt and this is how he generally analyses political upheavals.

Is there any wonder then, that the Congress dominated and controlled by the followers of Mr Gandhi would do everything in their power to crush the peasants' uprising? Keshav Menon and Madhav Menon, two prominent Congress-leaders of Malabar, did all that lay in their power to put a check to the uprising. Narayan Menon who was one of the leaders of the Tenancy movement, and later on cut off all connections with the Tenancy movement and had joined the Congress, moved about in the rebel areas with special passports issued by the government, in order to 'pacify' the rebels. Thousands of Moplahs came to meet him and accorded him a most hearty welcome, thinking that he had come to assist them. When they found that he had come to ask the rebel-leaders to stop fighting and to surrender themselves to the Police, one of the leaders remarked, 'we thought you have come to help us, now we realise you are against us'. One of the rebel-leaders whom Narayan Menon, prevailed upon to surrender to the police, requested him to leave that area as soon as possible as his life might be endangered if the peasants came to know about the reason of his visit. Narayan Menon returned happily, fulfilling his mission and the rebel leaders who surrendered to the police following his advice, were executed by the government. But such is the irony of historical justice that as a reward for his faithful services to the government, Narayan Menon was sentenced to twelve years imprisonment on the strength of the accusation by the same Police Inspector whose life he had saved from the hands of the rebels.

Gopala Menon, in those days a prominent Congress leader of Malabar, also went to the rebel-areas with the same object of helping the government to establish law and order. Describing to me the profound impression that the thousands of peasant-rebels had created on him, he said. 'It was worth one's while to take the chance, but consistent with my Gandhian principle I could not do that'. So, consistent with his Gandhian principles, Gopala Menon toured in the rebel-areas discouraging the rebels in their fight and persuading them to surrender to the government. Other minor Congress leaders also carried on the same noble mission with great zeal.

At least here, non-violence was practised by the followers of Mr Gandhi to perfection!

And Mr Gandhi had every reason to be sorry and he was more than right when in the article, 'The meaning of the Moplah rising', published in the *Young India*, on 20 October 1921, he wrote, 'I am sorry to believe, but it is my belief, that the men on the spot do not wish to give non-co-operators the credit for peacefully ending the trouble'.

The class-content of Gandhism, hidden behind the thin veil of non-violence, manifested itself in all its ugliness. Terrified by the reality of mass-upheaval, horror-stricken by the method of swift Justice that the peasants meted out to the spies and informers who happened to be Hindus, alarmed out of their wits by the jacquerie started by the peasants in the estates of the landlords who in this case were also Hindus through mere chance, the Gandhist Congress-leaders of Malabar used the dogma of non-violence as a plea to sabotage the uprising. Moreover, they spared no pains to prove that the uprising was communal in character.

Class-interest, masquerading in the guise of non-violence and communalism came to the help of British Imperialism in which it rightly recognised its main support.

The peasants of Malabar paid dearly for their attempt to end a feudal tyranny which is supported by British Imperialism. For a period of five months, the unarmed peasant masses of Malabar fought against the forces of the Government, ultimately succumbing to the incomparably superior military power of British Imperialism, which was supported loyally by the Gandhists and by the landlords.

The Call and Warning of 1921

Communist Party of India[1]

It was on 20 August 1921 that the anti-imperialist struggle which came to be known as the Moplah Rebellion began in Tirurangadi and surrounding areas. In scale, it was unprecedented and has not been matched by any other struggle in Kerala's subsequent history. The Communist Party uses this occasion to renew the sacred memory of this valiant struggle, which showed that even poor, illiterate, and unarmed peasants can take up arms to fight well-resourced, hegemonic imperialism.

The Party remembers, with heartfelt pride, the valour of tens of thousands of brave Moplahs who heeded the call for struggle by the Congress and the Khilafat Committee, and came forward to oppose the 'Rule of the Devil'.

The Party salutes the Moplah peasants, who braved the guns of the white man's army and the Gorkha army, fought against the devilish actions of those armies for nearly four months, and took up arms to wage an organised fight against the British army in a struggle known as the 'Battle of Pookkottoor'.

The Communist Party views the oppressive rule of hegemonic imperialism – which hanged Moplahs to death as an example to all those who dare to fight against imperialist domination, which tormented thousands after sending them to prisons and to Andaman, which orphaned numerous Moplah families, which

---

[1] Resolution passed in Calicut, 18-19 August 1946.

engineered the 'Wagon Tragedy' that can only be compared to the barbarism of Hitler-fascism, and which turned the verdant, beautiful Moplah land into a desert — with boundless hatred, anger, and vengefulness.

The Party remembers with contempt the cowardly stand of the Congress leadership which denounced the Moplahs — who fought so bravely, and who endured such brutal repression — in the name of 'himsa' (violence) and 'religious fanaticism', and which used the excuse of 'ahimsa' (non-violence) to evade its duty to oppose imperialist repression.

The Party remembers with disgust the actions of the Moplah elites who refused to move even a little finger to save their own community from barbaric imperialist repression, and who instead earned money and positions by betraying the poor Moplahs to the military and the police.

The Party also remembers the inspiring life of the late Muhammad Abdu Rahiman Sahib, who opposed the cowardice of the Congress leadership and the treason of the Moplah elites, who was proud of the brave history of the Moplahs, and who worked to retain [in the Congress ranks] those who upheld the fighting legacy of 1921. The Party once again affirms the position of this former Kerala Pradesh Congress Committee president that 1921 is not the private property of the Moplahs, but the common treasure of all of Malabar, and that hence the struggle should be called 'Malabar Rebellion' rather than 'Moplah Rebellion'. The Party appeals to each Malayali to learn the history and lessons of this anti-imperialist struggle which took place 25 years ago in Kerala.

Whatever had led to the Moplah Rebellion in 1921 exist today as well. Just like then, this is also a time in the immediate aftermath of a terrible big war. Inflation, scarcity of commodities, and other miseries are agonising the people. Just like then, this time too, the political consciousness following a big war has begun making waves among the people. As a result of all these, strikes and other struggles are causing ferment among all sections of people.

Just like the struggle of the Moplahs of Malabar in 1921, struggles of all sections of people are going to take place everywhere in India. Just like what was done to the 'Moplah Rebellion' of 1921, hegemonic imperialism and the princely rulers who are its guards are preparing to repress the struggles of 1946-47 using fascist means. Just like in 1921, today too, the national leadership is prepared to oppose the anti-imperialist struggle in the name of ahimsa and so on.

Just like in 1921, today too, we are confronted with the danger that instead of leading a united struggle of all sections of people against imperialist domination, one community would fight against the other community, resulting in both communities turning into servants of imperialism.

Therefore, the Party appeals to the supporters of the Congress and the League, and to all patriots to learn the lessons of 1921. We request the League supporters to understand the dangers that will result if preparations are made to wage jihad against the Congress and the Hindus, as the League is doing now. We appeal to Congress supporters to recognise the dangers of the statements being made by leaders such as Pandit Nehru to the effect that the Congress government would suppress the League's agitation. At this juncture when all sections of people are rising up, instead of destroying imperialist domination by leading people's struggles, the leaders of the Congress and the League are compromising with hegemonic imperialism and opposing strikes and other mass struggles. We appeal to the leaders of the Congress and the League to end this policy of theirs.

The Party appeals to the many lakhs of common people in the Congress and the League to learn the lessons of 1921.We would like to bring to the notice of Congress supporters that the very Congress leaders who took the masses to the streets in the name of the August Revolution had forgotten revolution in 1921, and that they are running to serve Wavell today as well.[2] We appeal to the masses supporting the League to see what the leaders of the League — who say that they have declared open struggle against the British — did in Malabar in 1921, and how the leaders of the League across India are now grovelling to the Governor. The Party appeals to the masses supporting the Congress and the League to remember that if they are unable to change the policy that their leaders are following today — the policy of compromise with the British and quarrelling with each other — then the miseries that the Moplah land had to endure in 1921 would befall the whole of India.

The Party appeals to the leftists who are there in the Congress in an organised manner under the banner of Congress Socialist Party, the Forward Bloc etc., and to the leftists who work in the League in an unorganised fashion, to learn the lessons of 1921. We appeal to them to learn how a mass struggle would fail when it comes under the leadership of leaders who propagate religious hatred and who are anti-revolutionists, how the land would be destroyed when even a struggle that affects only one community is turned into a communal riot, and how the leaders' anti-revolutionary attitude and a struggle's communal character would benefit imperialism. We appeal to them to understand that if the leftists in the Congress, the League, and so on, come together with the communists to oppose the anti-revolutionary, compromising policy of today's political leaders, and to organise people's sentiments in favour of struggle, there are possibilities of a victorious revolution.

---

[2] August Revolution, launched on 8 August 1942, refers to the Quit India movement launched by the Indian National Congress, demanding that British rule in India be ended. Archibald Percival Wavell was the Viceroy and Governor-General of India from 1 October 1943 to 21 February 1947.

The Moplah Rebellion

E.M.S. Namboodiripad[1]

It is to the illiterate, backward Moplah of the Eranad and Valluvanad taluks that the honour goes of having raised the initial voice of protest against the oppression of the Jenmi. His very backwardness, his inability to see the might of the new State built up by the white man, his ignorance of the intricacies of the new legal concepts introduced by that State, made him rise individually against individual acts of oppression indulged in either by the Jenmi or by the new bureaucratic State. He did not organise himself and his brethren into a peasant movement; for, in his ignorance, he only saw a particular Jenmi or a particular official oppressing him; he could not see the Jenmi system or the bureaucracy which supported it. At the same time, he acted firmly against his own immediate oppressors because he was not sophisticated enough to submit himself to the new oppressive system. Between 1836 and 1898, as many as 45 cases of criminal action by Moplahs against Hindus are recorded in the Eranad, Western Valluvanad, and North Ponnani taluks (an area with a dominant Moplah population). The official historians of Malabar draw the conclusion that the Moplahs are a fanatical band of lawbreakers. The government have accordingly enacted special laws (*Moplah Outrages Act*) to protect the decent and law-abiding citizens from them.

[1] E.M.S. Namboodiripad, *A Short History of the Peasant Movement in Kerala*, 1943. Reprinted in *History, Society, and Land Relations. Selected Essays*, New Delhi: LeftWord Books, 2010.

A careful analysis, however, shows that 80 per cent of these crimes are those committed by Moplah tenants against Hindu Jenmis or their agents or servants or the Adhilgari (village headman) or a revenue official or a police party. And remember that almost all the Jenmis in this area are Hindus — Nambudiris, Rajahs, and Temples particularly — and most of the tenants are Moplahs.

It is not, of course, denied that a certain percentage of the crimes are of a purely fanatical type. There are, for instance, cases of Cheruma (Harijan) converts having been attacked by bands of Moplahs for having reconverted themselves to Hinduism. Such instances are, for one thing, very rare, and, for another, we should remember that Moplah priests are working with the deliberate purpose of clouding the vision of the Moplah peasants. It is to the interests of these priests to turn the anti-Jenmi sentiments of the peasants into the anti-Hindu sentiments of the Moplahs. And it is no wonder that the backward Moplah fell victim to this propaganda. The wonder is, rather, that such fanatical outbursts are so few in proportion to their anti-Jenmi and anti-official actions. It clearly shows that with all his traditional illiteracy, backwardness, and priest-riddenness, the Moplah peasant is much more a class-conscious peasant than a community-conscious Moplah.

NINETEENTH CENTURY CIVILIANS WHO SPOKE UP

The latter half of the nineteenth century is remarkable in Indian history of the rise of a type of civilian who became the mouthpiece of the rising national movement. One of these, A.O. Hume, is supposed to be the Father of the Indian National Congress. He saw the necessity of creating an organisation which would prove a safety-valve for the rising national sentiment and confine it within safe limits.

The same tendency is visible in Malabar — not in her national politics but in her agrarian movement. It was Mr Logan, a civil servant, who first gave form to the anti-Jenmi sentiments of the people of Malabar. His report on the causes of Moplah outbreaks (into which he was commissioned to enquire) and the historical chapter of the *Malabar Manual* which he prepared at the government's instance are two classical documents bearing on the agrarian question in Malabar. They are quoted and re-quoted even today by the supporters of tenancy reform while the opponents of that reforms have taken great pains (with very little success) to refute them. A few more civilians followed in Logan's footsteps, while some took the other side and opposed any change in the tenancy system. But none of them — neither supporters nor opponents — equalled Logan in the penetrating analysis of Malabar society before and after the advent of the British regime. What were Mr Logan's chief conclusions?

1) That the British jurists did not understand the system of landownership in Malabar. They imported conceptions of the British feudal system and absolute property rights into Malabar, thus clothing the old indigenous terms and expressions denoting landed property with a new and alien meaning.

2) That there was no absolute proprietorship in land in Malabar. The Jenmi was only a co-proprietor with two classes of cultivators — tenants and agricultural labourers. His rights are limited to taking one third of the produce as jenmabhogam — which is not rent in the British sense of the word. He cannot raise the jenmabhogam above this one-third, nor can he evict his tenant from the land.

3) That the decisions of Courts making the Jenmi absolute owner, the right of eviction at will and with the right of taking as much rent as he can, were a wrong interpretation of the law.

4) They were also a social and political blunder of the first

magnitude. They are the real reasons for the Moplah outbreaks.

5) The solution is to restore the tenants to their old position, i.e., give them fixity of tenure, fix rent at old rates, and give compensation for tenants' improvements.

RISE OF THE KANAMDAR

Meanwhile a new force was slowly evolving in Malabar society. Out of the womb of this old feudal society emerged the elements of the new bourgeois society and this gave a new form, a new leadership, and an organisation to the hitherto unorganised peasant movements.

The Rajahs and the Sthanis (chieftains) formed the political superstructure of the old, pre-British society while the Namboodiris and religious institutions formed its cultural superstructure. The British regime gave a stunning blow to both and constructed a new superstructure politically and culturally. British power, however, kept the elements of the old superstructure intact as the base of its own economic superstructure. The contradictions involved in this gave birth to a new class — the rising bourgeoisie — and laid the basis for a great social upheaval.

It was the middle strata of the old society that constituted the cadres of the new political and cultural machine. The Rajahs, Sthanis, and Namboodiris did not take up English education and secure administrative posts. They held on to their economic and social predominance and pooh-poohed the alien tongue. It was their dependents, tenants and poor relatives that went to schools, passed examinations, and secured government posts.

Now this created a new situation. The new class of educated young men and officers were politically and culturally far more advanced than their landlords who, however, were economically and socially dominant in the countryside. The very State which made them politically independent of the Jenmis made them much more dependent economically on those same Jenmis.

A Tehsildar or a Police Inspector or a Sub-Judge is part of a machine which deals with Jenmis as with any other citizen, but individuals who are appointed to these posts are socially and economically dependent on some of these Jenmis. The officer has innumerable opportunities of bossing over the Jenmis as over the rest of the people, but the Jenmi can evict his family from the house in which it lives. The educated and professional man with a wide outlook and a sturdy sense of self-respect must humiliate himself before the narrow-minded and conceited ignoramus who is the landlord.

It was this conflict between the new rising bourgeoisie and the old decaying Jenmi that gave a new leadership to the peasant movement. The most outstanding individual of this type is the late Sir C. Sankaran Nayar. The slogans and demands of this class, however, were very different from those raised by Mr Logan. They, of course, quoted Logan when it was a question of refuting the arguments of the Jenmis, but they did not demand what Logan had demanded.

Now to get a clear understanding of the difference, it is necessary to bear in mind that there are two main classes of tenants in Malabar. One of these is called kanamdar, who had certain privileges, pays less rent, and has invested a small sum with the Jenmi. The other is verumpattamdar with no privileges, paying the full rent and cultivating on a theoretically year-to-year basis. Many of the kanamdars are themselves not cultivators, but lease their lands to verumpattamdars for cultivation, while most of the verumpattamdars are actual cultivators. All the kanamdars are thus directly under the Jenmis while verumpattamdars are both under the Jenmis and the kanamdars. It was thus the kanamdar, the prosperous middle tenant, that formed the soil out of which grew the rising bourgeoisie. While many kanamdars remained on the land as actual tillers of the soil, there were few, among the other classes — either Jenmis or verumpattamdars — who rose to the position of the new bourgeoisie. Thus, the struggle of the kanamdar for economic equality with the Jenmi was the struggle of the bourgeoisie for domination all along the line. This domination naturally necessitated that the verumpattamdar should not have equality with the kanamdar. The rich kanamdar did not mind equality of the poor kanamdar with the Jenmi but he did object to the verumpattamdar being equal to himself. So, the slogan was 'Fixity of Tenure for the Kanamdar'. Logan had, however, recommended no concessions to the kanamdar, but only to the verumpattamdar.

This struggle was bitter and prolonged. It took over half a century (from the latter part of the last century to 1930) to see the end of the struggle in which the kanamdar emerged victorious. The struggle was not confined to British Malabar but took the same form and intensity in the States of Cochin and Travancore where, however, the struggle ended more than a decade before it did in British Malabar. The chequered history of their struggle by means of reports and memoranda, brochures and tracts, newspaper articles and platform oratory, petitions and counterpetitions, draft-bills and debates, committees and conferences, vetoes, and recommendations at last resulted in three separate Acts for the three separate political divisions of the Malayalam speaking area. All this need not be detailed here. Sufficient to say that the Malabar tenancy question was as recurrent and persistent a subject in Madras for half a century as the Irish question was (for four centuries) in London. And yet its solution did not touch the fringe of the problem even as the Anglo-Irish treaty has not touched the fringe of the British colonial problem. What is more, the solution of the tenancy question in 1930 had to be preceded by the Rebellion of 1921 even as the settlement of the Irish question in 1921 had to be preceded by the Easter Rising of 1916. We will, therefore, now refer to this historic rising which was the fiercest struggle against the British authority since 1857.

THE COURSE OF THE REBELLION

It is the fashion among certain 'Marxist' circles (e.g., Soumyendra Nath Tagore's *Peasant Revolt in Malabar*) to speak of the 1921 rebellion as a purely peasant uprising against the Jenmis. Facts, however, tell a different tale. What is more, these 'Marxists' seem to disregard the clear warning of Engels against applying the theory of historical materialism as if it were 'easier than the solution of a simple equation of the first degree'. Engels says:

According to the materialist conception of history the determining element in history is ultimately the production and reproduction in real life. More than this neither Marx nor I have ever asserted. If therefore somebody twists this into the statement that the economic element is the only determining factor, he transforms it into a meaningless abstract and absurd phrase. There is an interaction of all these elements (political, legal, philosophical theories, religious ideas, etc.) in which amid all the endless bursts of accidents (i.e., of things and events whose interaction is so remote or so impossible to prove that we regard it as absent and can neglect it) the economic movement finally asserts itself [Engels to J. Bloch, 21 September 1890].

Now there is no doubt about the fact that it was the anti-Jenmi struggle of the Malabar peasants that gave birth to the great mass upheaval of 1920–21 which resulted in the five months' rebellion in South Malabar. Since this is not a detailed history of the 1921 rebellion (which, unfortunately, is yet to be written apart from those booklets by official apologists) I cannot give here the innumerable facts and figures to refute the lies and slanders of those who would have us believe that the Moplahs as a community are undesirable lawbreakers. I would quote the late C. Gopalan Nair, a government pensioner who wrote a booklet on the rebellion defending the official view. It may be stated that this booklet has been commended to the reader by no less a person than the then Collector of Malabar.

The house of V. Mohammed, the local Khilafat Secretary, was searched by the police for a gun alleged to have been stolen from the Pookttur Palace of the Nilambur Thirumulpad and this gave the Moplahs the opportunity for which they were waiting, of asserting the authority and force of the Khilafat movement. On the pretext that the search was unjust and uncalled for, a crowd of several hundred of Moplahs armed with knives, swords, and spears, collected with astounding rapidity and advanced to the Palace. It transpired that they had been summoned from various neighbouring and outlying villages by a tocsin of drums beaten in local and neighbouring mosques. They levied blackmail from the landlords on threat of murder and also threatened to murder the Circle Inspector or Police who recognized the necessity of dealing tactfully . . .

No evidence has yet been forthcoming to warrant the allegation regarding agrarian discontent, but it would appear that there was some trouble — what it was, it is not possible to say — between Pookottur Moplahs and the Manager Thirumulpad of the Pookottur Estate. Their lack of cordiality was aggravated by the police search instituted at the instance of the manager and V. Mohammed exploited the Khilafat Movement and the factious temper of his co-religionists to wreak vengeance. The Moplahs demanded their wages at 9 o'clock that night, threatened the manager and became turbulent. And in this jungly, remote and fanatical hamlet of Pookottur, the civil administration practically ceased to function from 2 August 1921 (pp. 21–23).

On page 30, he says: 'In the realm of industry, the Moplah has no rival, his good qualities in ordinary life are admitted; during the rebellion several instances have occurred of Moplahs having helped Hindus to escape, but individual instances do not prove the rule'.

The short biographical sketches that he gives on pages 76–80 of some of the rebel leaders are illuminating.

Wariankunnath Kunhammad Haji, of a family of outbreak traditions, as a lad was transported with his father for complicity in a previous outbreak; on his return 6 or 7 years ago, he was not allowed to settle down in his native village but after a time he went up to his village and started life as a cartman. On the introduction of the Khilafat movement, he joined it and became one if its chief workers, organized Sabhas and became the guiding spirit of the Khilafat in Eranad. On the outbreak of the rebellion, he became King, celebrated his accession by the murder of Khan Bahadur Chekkutty, a Moplah retired Police Inspector. He styled himself as the Raja of the Hindus, Amir of the Mohammedans and Colonel of the Khilafat Army. He wore a fez cap, wore the Khilafat uniform and badge and he had sword in his hand. He enjoyed absolute Swaraj in his kingdom of Eranad and Valluvanad. He announced that he was aware that the inhabitants have suffered from robbing and looting, that he would impose no taxation on them this year (1921) save in the way of donations to the yudha [war] fund and that next year the taxes must be forthcoming. He ordered members of agricultural labourers to reap and bring in the paddy raised in the Thirumulpad's lands, the harvesters being paid in cash and the grain set apart to feed the Haji's forces. He issued passports to persons wishing to get outside his Kingdom and the cost of the pass was a very flexible figure, according to the capacity of the individual concerned. 'He was captured on the 6th January and shot on 20th January, 1922.

This was the most outstanding of the rebel leaders. Now about two of the lesser ones:

Seethi Koya Thangal of Kumarampathur set himself up as the Governor of a Khilafat principality. He issued fatwas warning his men against looting, and other depredations pointing out that the country had become theirs. Three of the rioters implicated in Elampalasseri were punished by him holding his own court-martial. The offenders were ordered to be shot, taking care only to use blank cartridges. The men terrified fell down. When they rose there were no injuries which the Thangal attributed to his own marvellous powers and added that his men will similarly be immune from British military attacks. He was captured and shot.

Chembrasseri Imbichi Koya Thangal held his court about midway between Tirur and Karuvarakundu on the slope of a bare hillock with about 4,000 followers from neighbouring villages. More than 40 Hindus were taken to the Thangal with their hands tied behind their back, charged with the crime of helping the military by supplying them with milk, tender coconuts, etc., and 38 of these were condemned to death. He superintended the work of murder in person and took his seat on a rock near a well, witnessed his men cutting at the necks of his victims and pushing the bodies into the well. 38 were murdered, one of whom a pensioned head-constable, to whom he owed a grudge, had his head neatly divided into two halves. Surrendered at Melattur and shot on 20th January, 1922.

FORCES BEHIND THE OUTBREAK

What then was the main force which led to the outbreak of 1921? The so-called Marxists would say that it was agrarian discontent. Nor do I wish to contradict it. Had it not been for the agrarian discontent whose causes and extent had been correctly stated by Mr Logan half-a-century ago but whose remedy was not applied by the government, the Moplah would not have rallied round the Khilafat and Congress flags in such large numbers and with such firm determination. It should also be remembered that most of the Congress and Khilafat leaders in Malabar (e.g., late K. Madhavan Nair, U. Gopala Menon, K.P. Kesava Menon, etc.) were also leaders of the Tenancy movement. The two most controversial resolutions considered and ultimately passed at the Malabar district Political Conference held at Manjeri were those supporting non-cooperation and Tenancy Reform. And it was after this Conference that Congress and Khilafat Committees sprang up in South Malabar in such large numbers as were not rivalled even in 1938–40.

Every speech of every Congress-cum-Khilafat leader was a two-edged weapon aimed against both the British Government as well as the Jenmi. It was this that gave a new hope and new slogan to the oppressed Moplahs who joined the movement in such large numbers. It was a fine example of an agrarian political mass movement.

The 'Marxists', however, have to answer certain simple but relevant questions. Why was it that the movement was confined to an area with a Moplah majority? The British bureaucracy and the Jenmi system which it set up cannot be said to be partial towards the Hindu peasants who are as numerous in other taluks as the Moplahs are in Eranad and parts of Valluvanad and Ponnani. The oppression and exploitation of the Jenmi and the officials are as bad for the Hindu peasants as for their Moplah comrades. Why is it then that Moplah peasants rose almost to a man while the Hindu peasants fell victims to the propaganda that the rising was not anti-Jenmi or anti-government but anti-Hindu? For it cannot be denied that the Hindus as a whole kept aloof from the rebellion and were far behind the Moplahs in the pre-rebellion period of agitation and organization. The number of Congress and Khilafat sabhas organised and members enrolled in the Moplah area, was far higher than the corresponding number in other areas. And finally, why was it that a certain number of forced conversions took place, which as I have remarked before, cannot by any stretch of imagination be explained away as part of a purely agrarian movement?

I have posed the question which every Marxist historian worth the name should answer. I do not, however, pretend to answer them here. It requires much better and more careful study than I have been able to give to the subject. But the little study that I have made has led me to certain conclusions which I set forth below:

1) The Moplahs as a community have a much higher sense of organisation than the Hindus. Their congregational prayers, their common feasts and dinners, their conception of equality among themselves, etc., make them much more amenable to organised work than their brethren of other communities. So, when the message of organization and struggle was preached by political leaders, the Moplahs took it much more easily and with much firmer determination than others.

2) The Moplahs had more reason to rally round the Congress and Khilafat than the Hindus. For, one of the slogans raised by the nationalist leadership was 'hands off the Turkish Khalifa', a slogan dear to the hearts of every pious Muslim. While for the Hindu peasant it was only a question of freedom from bureaucracy and the Jenmi, it was to the Moplah a question of defending his religious head, a question of sacred war against the desecrator of his creed.

3) While the above two reasons give adequate explanation for the more solid organisation in the Moplah area, they do not explain the course which the rebellion took. This is much more complex a question than the one answered above.

4) The key to the whole question as to the course of the

rebellion is supplied by the different strata of society which rallied by the Congress cum-Khilafat-cum-Tenancy movement. These can be divided as follows:

a) The Hindu elements of the central leadership in Malabar. They were vakils and intellectuals drawn from among the kanamdars. They were the typical bourgeois nationalist leadership. Furious against the bureaucracy, earnest about the struggle against it, elated at the staggering response to their call for struggle, sanguine about their own ability to control the masses within the four corners of nonviolent non-cooperation, indignant against oppressive Jenmi yet blind to the demands and aspirations of the verumpattamdars, they went forth to the masses with the message of organisation for a struggle. They were with and among the masses, till the latter began to adopt the creed of non-violence and then left them to their fate.

b) The Moplah elements of the same leadership. Closely akin to their Hindu counterparts, but with firmer roots in the masses, they stood for the verumpattamdars, and were therefore more progressive. They did not leave the masses, but tried to bring them into the limits of non-violent non-cooperation. The most outstanding of these, Mr Mohammed Abdur Rahman, is even today the hero of the Moplahs.

c) The middle leadership in the rebel area consisted mainly of Musaliars, Thangals, Hajis and other saintly Moplahs. Sincere antiimperialists, they, however, think and speak in the terms of religion which had tremendous effect in rallying the Moplahs. Some of them have had the adventurous and the careerist in them, but most of them were good material as peasant cadres if only there had been a good and efficient central leadership. Their loss is irreparable to the peasant movement as they showed their mettle as good organisers both before and during the rebellion.

d) Rank and Filers. These may have naturally included a certain percentage of unsocial and individualist elements but most of them were typical anti-Jenmi and, therefore, anti-government peasants.

e) Hindu elements of middle leadership and rank and filers were on the same pattern as their leaders and left the movement altogether after the outbreak and the arrival of the military.

f) It is not difficult to explain now why the movement in its later stages took a partially communal turn. The Moplah found that his Hindu compatriots, both the leaders and the rank and file, deserted him; the military arrived to hunt him out of his abode; his Hindu neighbours helped the military against him. He naturally got enraged at them. This was worked upon by fanatical and adventurous elements among the rebels. No wonder then if anti-Hindu actions took place. The wonder is, rather, that they were so few in number and proportion.

It was thus that the greatest mass movement in British Malabar was diverted into the most tragic and most futile mass action. Did anybody divert it deliberately and, if so, who, is a question for a penetrating study of facts, but one can definitely say that behind the whole tragedy can be seen the colossal ignorance of the central political leadership in Malabar and India as to the actual character of the mass force roused by them. The leaders got a following of a very different character from what they wanted, yet thought it was what they wanted. South Malabar had to wade through blood and get its civil liberties suppressed for over a decade in order to learn that leadership is not all-powerful nor the masses a herd of sheep. Thousands of lives had to be lost and many more to suffer untold privations because the masses had an organisation of their own but a different type of leadership.

The Direct Action Lessons of 1921

A.K. Gopalan[1]

Friends, I have so far spoken mainly on the purpose of celebrating this day. I propose now to speak only about some doubts relating to it. There have been several movements in this country at different times for winning the freedom of this country. As regards 9 August, it is said that we should recall to our minds the events that have happened in this country since 9 August. For, several things have taken place in this country for the freedom of this land. We have not forgotten the happenings after 9 August 1942 for the freedom of this country. Likewise, we have not forgotten that four comrades of Kayyur were hanged. So also, we have not forgotten the execution of Bhagat Singh. Many people of this country have been locked up in jails. We have not forgotten that women and men of this country have been shot dead. The Jallianwala Bagh massacre took place in this country some years ago. A European gentleman Dyer shot and killed several people of this country at a place called Jallianwala Bagh. When that gentleman was asked why he stopped shooting he replied that the ammunition had run out. We have not forgotten that. Similarly, Bhagat Singh was hanged. Some time ago, British imperialism sent to the gallows four patriots known as the Kayyur comrades. We know about all

[1] On 25 August 1946, AKG gave this speech at a public meeting in Perinthalmanna. He was arrested and jailed. It was from jail that he followed the independence of India. The speech is from the court proceedings, the transcript done for the Home Department on April 25, 1947 (Kozhikode Archives).

those. We cherish all those who courted imprisonment in this country for the sake of freedom as patriots.

Twenty-five years ago, there arose from our folk an ordinary Muslim — Ali Musliyar — who for the country's freedom carried on a mighty struggle in Kerala against British rule, against slavery and injustice. If for the freedom of this country anybody in Kerala had been able to put up a bold fight against the British empire, if anybody in Kerala can claim to be brave and determined, it is these brave and poor Muslim peasants, who facing guns and cannons, defied the white soldiers and even their mechanised divisions as if they didn't care a straw for them, and carried on a brave struggle for freedom. These Moplah brethren of ours, we should never forget. The August revolution consisted of pulling down telegraph wires, removing rails, and burning of police stations, but the Moplah friends of Malabar under Ali Musliyar and Wariankunnath Kunhammad Haji had a brave encounter with white troops at the place called Pookkoottur. The British imperialist government had guns, cannons, planes, and ships, but whatever they may have had, our brave Mappila brethren courageously, prepared themselves to fight, saying that they had the strength and courage for it. Those unarmed Muslim friends openly fought the white troops and established their rule in two taluks of Malabar for nearly three months. They expelled the British empire from that place and ordinary peasants and labour friends carried on the administration there. They put this into operation for about three months in 1921. It was Ali Musliyar who did it. They demonstrated that if the people of two taluks join together, not all the Gurkha troops, white troops, the police and the officials together will be able to oppress them. Our unity gave us so much strength. Without guns, without planes, without spears, Ali Musliyar was able to rule for nearly three months.

Without remembering that, we shall not be fit for the struggle for freedom. Without realising its merit, you will not be able to conduct a mighty struggle for the freedom of the country. That is why we speak and feel proud of 1921. Whoever you may be, whether Hindu or Muslim, if you are anti-imperialist and if you feel that this incompetent British rule should be ended, you should learn the lesson of the brave struggle carried on by the patriotic youth of this country in 1921. Without studying the circumstances of that struggle very well, it will not be possible to put into execution your direct action. It will not be possible to put an end to British rule. That is why we say that the good lesson of 1921 should be learnt.

The Moplah friends of this country were not BAs [Bachelor of Arts] in those days. They did not have much school education either. They did not carry the Khan Bahadur title. But they were brave men. They did not make speeches in those days for the freedom of the country. But they faced the guns, they faced cannons, they faced the officials, and they demonstrated that guns and weapons are all as straw before the might of people. They were able to rule for three months. Can this be forgotten? Does this not deserve to be commemorated? This is what we must ask the Congress friends who sing the praises of the August revolution.

What we have to say is this: that if the Direct Action launched by the Muslim League of 15 August is to be a real action it should be directed against the British empire. We want to tell Muslim League leaders that if they want to carry on Direct Action against the British empire, they should learn well the lesson of the struggle from 1921. That was the right struggle. There was direct action in Kerala in 1921. It should not be forgotten. Every year you should recall the struggle of 1921. The struggle carried on by the people of this place who may be reckoned in crores, in thousands, our Muslim brethren, for the freedom of this country against the oppression of the landlords and the wagon tragedy that took place in that struggle ought not to be forgotten.

Therefore, we say it is 1921 that we are observing. In 1921 the people carried a direct action, an armed revolt for the freedom of this country, for ending the hardships borne by people, for affording protection to the folk of this country from Jenmis, and for putting an end to the acts of highhandedness resorted to by the police, the officials, and the Jenmis. While speaking of the armed revolt of 1921, let me ask our Congress friends who lay much stress on non-violence what the August revolution was. It was cutting of wires, removal of rails. High-handed officials had been attacked. Some of them had died. Was it non-violent? Even Pandit Nehru says that we should remember the August revolution. If the Congress considers that the August revolution is a struggle against the British Empire, then why do they not commend or keep up the memory of the struggle of 1921 similarly. There are certain reasons to refer to that Malabar rebellion as they do. When thousands of Muslims prepared to die for the freedom of this country that campaign happened to be characterised in that manner only on account of anti-Muslim feeling.

The government of these days (Khilafat) was a government of the poor. It was a government by the labourers and peasants. Those who belonged to the camp of Wariankunnath Kunhammad Haji were peasants. There were rich people there. There were capitalists. But who was carrying on the administration? Wariankunnath Kunhammad Haji, a poor cart man, a man who had not passed any examination. But he was the leader of the people, the leader of the poor. Officials who were BAs and MAs [Master of Arts] saluted him. He gave orders to them. There were no officials taking bribes. The poor got protection. Judges, whether Hindu or Muslim, gave decrees without communal bias. There were several stories of poor people receiving protection irrespective of their being Hindus or Muslims from the government of Wariankunnath Kunhammad Haji. He said to officials:

You are educated people. You are people who take bribes. But under my government, the British way of administration is not enough. You should not take bribes. Wariankunnath Kunhammad Haji is ruling the country. Therefore, the people should be protected.

We are said to be stirring up riots between Hindus and Muslims. No man of sense, no patriot will stir up riots between Hindus and Muslims. We do stir up riots, but they are not communal riots. Riots against whom then? Against this useless British rule. We are inciting the people of the country to rebel against those rulers who think that they have guns and swords, killed poor Muslims in what was known as the Wagon Tragedy. Hindus and Muslims should not cut each other's throats.

None of the theories of non-violence will prevail hereafter. If the people as a whole make up their minds to resist the acts of highhandedness from whatever quarter this may come, whether from police, capitalists, or Jenmis, it will certainly be possible to put an end to them in this country quickly. And it will not be possible to live comfortably. Therefore, when I mention 1921, when I ask you to celebrate its anniversary, that is to say the Pookoottur Day, you shout *zindabad* to our Moplah brethren of 1921. If there have been great patriots in this country, they are those Moplah brethren. We will keep alive the memory of those who in 1921 for the sake of this country's freedom got ready to fight before the British guns and rifles, fighting injustice and highhandedness of landlords and officials. Then many of the good youth of this land braved soldiers' guns in the cause of this country's freedom.

You and I have not done such a thing so far. It may be that we have given lectures, courted imprisonment, and claimed to be brave. When rifles and cannons are fired, how many do you think there would be to march forward against them unarmed, seize the cannon, and fight back? Only very few. When such brave men waged an antiimperialist struggle for the sake of their country, and with a view to put an end to the excesses of landlords and the police, that was the right struggle, the memory of which we should keep alive. We will say this a hundred times. We will say it even if we are hanged for it. For, if anybody deserves to be called patriots, if anybody has done real fighting, if people have fought for this country with unflinching courage, such patriots are our Moplah brethren. There is no doubt about it. The Congressmen who do not think of it are not patriots. Many good people faced the gun and met with their death in the cause of the country's freedom. Remember them.

Our people should copy the good features of that struggle and be careful to avoid the wrong ones. There will be no riots at the bidding of the communist. Who is there to stir up riots? It is Pandit Nehru. He said to the League recently: 'either you will perish or we'. It is not we, that incite people to riots. It is the Congress leaders and League leaders. They are interested in doing it. We are not. For among communists, there is no Jenmi, no capitalist, no rich man. In the Muslim League there are capitalists and Jenmis. So also, in the Congress. At Calicut, Badushah Sahib evicts poor Muslim tenants from several houses. A capitalist is a capitalist, whoever he may be, whether Samuel Aron or Bathal Sait, Hindu or Muslim, Congress or League. The object of the capitalist is to extract work out of the poor people of this country, to whichever religion they may belong, to pay them minimum wages and to make starve their family. The Congress capitalist and League capitalist, the Congress Jenmi and League Jenmi are creating splits between the Congress labourer and League labourers, between Hindu labourers and Muslim labourers and between the poor Hindu folk and Muslim folk to serve their selfish interests for the British capitalists and Indian capitalists are at loggerheads with each other. The Indian capitalist thinks: 'I want the Railway. The British capitalist should not be allowed to plunder the poor people of the country wholesale. I too must have a share'. The field of exploitation should not be left exclusively to the British. The Congress and League capitalists say that they too want to exploit.

If anybody in this country has waged an anti-imperialist

struggle for the freedom of this country, if anybody has resorted to direct action it was in 1921 and it was by the Moplah friends of Eranad and Valluvanad taluks. At the same time one or two things should not be forgotten: that is the difference between 1921 and 1946. In 1921, the country was in a difficult plight that followed the great World War of 1914-18. There was trouble. There was a shortage of rice. Cloth was not available. Further, the new Khilafat Movement had been launched. The Hindus and Muslims had been organised as one body. In 1946, just see what has been happening in the country for the last eight months or one year. Indians of the Indian navy, not only Moplahs, but all people, one morning removed the union jack from their ships and foisted the Congress and the League flags in its place and told the Britisher: 'You must quit India. We should be given the same pay as is being given to the whites'. So, saying, they started direct action.

You must take note of the fact that even British troops strike work for our freedom. The MSP. [Malabar Special Police] struck work; they struck work saying that they were not prepared to go about all over the country and shoot and beat people for Rs. 21. Two thousand men of MSP who had struck work were dismissed by the government. The day before yesterday it was seen from the newspaper that the reserve police at Tinnevelly had struck work. Thus, policemen struck work; postal employees struck work; 10 lakhs of railway workers said that they were prepared to strike work. Then the government said that a compromise should be reached. Now, the non-gazetted officers who had been till now wearing coats and ties are now going about in Madras shouting *zindabad*. Officers, except the European Collector, government officials drawing salaries of Rs. 200 and Rs.300, the police and MSP, are ready to strike work. Why? Is striking work rioting? It is no longer possible to suffer the increasing pangs of hunger. Riot has broken out in the stomach of the starving. All these strikes are the consequences of people having been driven mad by hunger. There are no riots except such riots.

Why are we shadowed? They are going to arrest us. We are being prosecuted. Black marketing is going on daily. There is no prosecution. Now people say, 'Please do not ask us to detect black marketing. We detected black marketing and now black marketers take revenge on us'. Pandit Nehru said that black marketers should be hanged. One need not go to the extent of hanging them. Will they be punished? Alagappa Chettiyar was caught when taking four lakhs of rupees worth of cloth to the black market. Was he punished? What, then, is the government for? Jenmies and capitalists should be punished. The government should have no fears in that matter. When railway employees strike work, the police and MSP should not be sent against them. There should be strength and courage enough not to send the police to the help of a capitalist European. If you cannot do good, will you refrain from doing devil? This is our only request to Congress. We have respect for the Congress. We are called traitors to the country. Have we not taken part in the Congress movement? But today we are not in the Congress. Today, Muthiah Chettiar is the Congress representative. What will happen if Muthiah Chettiar goes to rule the country? Black markets! The Rajah of Bobbili sent an elephant to trample on a meeting addressed by Srimathi Sarojini Naidu. And today, he has been selected by the Congress as its representative. The Congress does not want us.

In 1946, the whole country is prepared to do anything to win freedom. But the Congress and the League must give the lead. Instead, the Congress and the League stand apart, like bitter enemies. If the Congress says that it is daytime now the League will say that it is night. You must unite. Are you not the people of this country? Can you not unite against the British? The Congress and League belong to this country. Why cannot they unite?

You should honour those Muslim brethren who in 1921 died for the freedom of the country. You must proclaim them as brave men who laid down their lives for the cause of freedom. Do you love your country? Are you enemies of British imperialism? If so, respect those people who fought then. You should not forget Wariankunnath Kunhammad Haji. He ruled the country for about three months. Though the British were here, no European had gone to that land for three months. Haji knew how to carry on the administration. It must be done without harassing the people and without taking bribes. He said that government should be for the good of the people. The Congress and League should realise this. The lesson of those days should be learnt.

The British government is our common enemy. The Congress and League should not fight between themselves. Calcutta is a striking instance in point. Saying that they are against the government, Hindus and Muslims fight against each other. Damages have been estimated to the tune of 5 crores of rupees. It is said that a large number of people have died. Congressmen and Leaguers cannot walk on the roads. The white soldier walks the roads smoking a cigar. The Britisher walks along the streets of Calcutta trampling on your dead bodies. Will the Congress leaders and League leaders learn this lesson? Why do people strike work? Is it at the bidding of communists that persons getting salaries of Rs. 300 strike work? It is impossible for men to get on. There are the haves and have nots, the capitalist and the labourer, the Jenmi and the peasant in this country. Strikes are the result.

People do not get a living wage. They insist on getting it. You people must say: 'Oh leaders, we have great respect for you, but if you do not care to unite, we shall unite, the poor labourers and peasants will unite. And then we shall carry on the affairs of the country'. This is what you should say. Otherwise, the anti-imperialist struggle will become an internecine struggle and our people will fail to get freedom.

There will be unemployment in the land. There will be scarcity of cloth and rice. We shall not get anything. This is the lesson of 1921. If there be any aggression today, it will not be 1921 that will follow, but 1946. In the present railway strike, it is direct action that we are going to carry out. We shall return blow for blow.

If there be need to resort to arms, we shall take up arms also. Otherwise, mere satyagraha is not going to achieve anything here. Did you not see what we got by the satyagraha of Gandhiji and the Congress? We must be prepared to conduct an organised struggle, an armed struggle like the one that took place in 1921. If violence is necessary, it should be used. Only those who are prepared for it, need come forward. The British government resorts to violence. Then why should we not use violence? I do not at all believe in non-violence. If anyone has faith in it, let him go and pursue that method. We take the lesson of the struggle of 1921. Thereby it will be possible to bring the British empire to its knees. Did not Kunhammad Haji rule over two taluks for three months? Muslim peasants ruled the country. No BA degree holder is necessary to rule the country. Comrade Ishaq is not necessary. It is the rule of the peasants that is coming.

The organised struggle of 1921 is direct action. We congratulate ourselves on it. It is only by such struggle that the freedom of the country can be won. But we must take particular care to see that it does not become a communal riot. If a united struggle is launched, riots of the kind that occurred in Calcutta cannot happen. To avoid such riots, the leaders of the League and the Congress should advise the people. The facts of the situation should be explained to them. I do not have much more to speak to you now. I have explained to you the object of this meeting. Some further accounts of this will be found in the columns of the *Deshabhimani*. People should purchase the copies of that paper and read the paper. It is not our object to stir up communal riots. We advise people that the whole country should remember those Moplah brethren who died for freedom.

Reflections on the Peasants' Revolt of 1921-22 in Malabar

Subhashini Ali[1]

A hundred years ago, in September 1921, the Non-Cooperation-Khilafat Movement was launched by Gandhiji all over India. People were exhorted to withdraw co-operation from the British Government. Gandhiji had toured the length and breadth of the country, often accompanied by either Maulana Mohammad Ali or Maulana Shaukat Ali. The demand for restoration of the Khilafat, which the British victory over Turkey in the First World War had brought to an end, was tagged onto the call for Non-Cooperation by Gandhiji in order to draw Muslim masses into the movement. Their enthusiastic participation, not only because of the Khilafat demand, saw a tremendous display of Hindu-Muslim unity in many parts of the country, a unity that spelt a great threat to the British government.

It was in a part of the Malabar region of what is now Kerala that the demand for Khilafat evinced the greatest response from the local Muslims known as Moplahs. The Kerala Moplahs have a history very different from that of other Muslim communities in India. They are descendants of Arabs engaged in trade along the Western coast who settled in Kerala and married local women. At one time, they controlled trading activities in the region but were, however, supplanted first by the Portuguese and then by the British. Members of a prosperous trading community, they had little

---

[1] An expanded article from *The Wire*, 21 November 2021.

choice but to become tenant farmers at the mercy of exploitative Namboodiri and Nair landlords. Many of them joined the British Army when the First World War broke out and were then cashiered in l918. They returned to the Malabar region of Kerala, which was part of the Madras Presidency at the time. They were well-trained soldiers, and they reacted to the cruel exploitation of Namboodiri and Nair landlords (Jenmis), who extracted many kinds of taxes and payments from them and also cancelled their tenancy at will, evicting them from the land that was then auctioned to others.

Interestingly, a gentleman by the name of Madhavan Nair, hailing from Malabar, wrote two detailed articles for the *Bombay Chronicle* on 19 September and 27 September 1921. In the first article, he writes, 'To those who have taken the trouble of understanding the Moplahs and understanding their history seriously, there is absolutely nothing surprising in the present troubles', and goes on to describe many smaller revolts that took place at the end of the 19th century and the beginning of the 20th and says that even in 1918 an attack on a landlord family took place by Moplah tenantry. He goes on to say that Mr Connolly, who was the Collector of Malabar at the time, was convinced that it was 'agrarian distress that was at the root of these troubles' and he made a strong representation to the government to intervene and end the injustices suffered by the tenants. It seems that the government set up a Commission. One of the things that the Commission mentioned was that the Thangal (Muslim religious head) of Theringeradi had a very powerful influence on many in the community and was 'a danger to public safety'. It was decided to exile him and his family to Arabia. More than 12,000 Moplahs gathered in protest and the Thangal admonished them that their behaviour was not in consonance with the tenets of their religion. Madhavan Nair says that thousands of weeping Moplahs accompanied the Thangal to the ship that was to take him and his family away, and he comforted them saying that they must not resort to violence.

Despite the Commission, nothing was done by the British government to end the miseries of the tenants, and Mr Nair writes, 'Moplahs, however, need no new reasons to break out into revolt'. According to him, the only difference between what happened in 1921 and what had occurred earlier was that the riots were more widespread and militant, and he attributes this to the Non-cooperation movement and also to the fact that large numbers of Moplahs had received military training in the British Indian Army. Mr Nair goes on to say, 'The immediate cause of every Moplah rising is the deplorable fact that in spite of repeated representations . . . the Madras Govt. have remained quite indifferent towards the untold sufferings of the peasantry of Malabar whom a set of barbarous laws has placed completely at the mercy of the Jenmis'. He goes on to describe these laws, which decided what the tenants could wear, what kind of homes they could live in, how they could marry, and so on.

After having asserted repeatedly in the two articles that it was agrarian distress that was at the root of the Moplahs' revolt, he says that while initially only landlords were attacked once the British army and administration subjected them to indescribable cruelty and violence, the nature of the movement changed, and 'crazed Moplahs' resorted to indiscriminate attacks on Hindu homes and temples.

Another report on the movement is to be found in the unfinished autobiography of a legendary freedom fighter who, after 1932, joined the Communist Party and died of torture at the hands of Congressmen and the police in jail in 1948.[2] Com. Sankaran was an active Congress organiser and leader of the Malabar region. He attended the Manjeri Conference organised by the Congress in March 1920 to launch the Non-cooperation movement in Malabar later in the year. He says that 'there were two reasons for the sheer level of energy exhibited at the meeting'. The first was that

---

[2] Moyarath Sankaran, *Autobiography of a Freedom Fighter and Martyr*, Trivandrum: Chintha Publishers, 2016.

Annie Besant had mobilised her supporters to oppose the Non-cooperation Resolution and 'two, the landlords had issued a dire threat against the moving or passing of the Tenant Resolution. If the meeting passed the resolution, they would oppose the non-cooperation movement tooth and nail'.

As a result, there was a huge mobilisation of the rural poor, including very large numbers of Moplahs, by those in favour of both resolutions, and they were passed 'with a thumping majority'. It is important to note that the all-India Khilafat meeting took place on 30 August 1921 and, in the course of their tours to promote the Khilafat agitation, Gandhiji and Maulana Shaukat Ali visited and addressed meetings in Malabar too. While the issue of Khilafat was important in mobilising Muslim support for the Non-cooperation Movement all over India, in Malabar, it seems from several reports like those of Madhavan Nair and Moyarath Sankaran that it was the issue of tenancy reform that galvanized Moplahs in Malabar. Since they were convinced that landlord oppression was aided and abetted in every way by the British government, it was only natural that they would wholeheartedly support the movement organised to challenge the British Empire itself. As Com. Moyarath Sankaran says 'The Muslim peasants believed that if British rule came to an end, the practise of paying rent to the Namboodiri landlords could be discontinued'.

While the non-cooperation movement elicited a big response in most parts of Malabar, the Moplahs from around Tirurangadi in Malabar were its most militant participants. The government retaliated with great severity, which only increased the resistance of the Moplahs, who soon 'liberated' a large area which remained under their control for some months. The brutality of British repression, the execution of several Moplah leaders, and the influence of religious leaders changed the course of the rebellion. E.M.S. Namboodiripad described the anarchy of the last days of the rebellion when communal attacks accompanied attacks against the British thus: 'the greatest mass movement in British Malabar was diverted into the most tragic and futile mass action'.[3]

The RSS has now seized upon the Malabar events to suit its political agenda. It has demanded that the names of many of the rebellion's martyrs' names be struck off the list of freedom fighters prepared decades ago by the Kerala Government. Its ideologues have published a rash of articles that describe the Moplah rebels as forerunners of the Taliban and go on to tar all Moplahs with this brush of Islamic fundamentalism. They are all, however, silent on the subject of British atrocities and the reign of terror that they instituted in Malabar after crushing the rebellion. As a result, the violence indulged in by some groups of Moplahs is ascribed to the myth propagated by the RSS that 'they' (Muslims) are 'like that', congenitally violent, and bloodthirsty.

Mozhikunnath Brahmadattan Namboodiripad was the President of the local Congress committee in his area of Valluvanad. He wrote an eye-witness account of the rebellion.[4] He, too, was an active Congress worker living adjacent to the epicentre of the revolt. He writes in his book that 'The root cause of the rebellion is not to be sought in communal conflict. It sprang out of political repression. Police atrocities provoked it. This rebellion is only an aspect of the freedom struggle'. M.B. Namboodiripad's book is important because he was not only a witness but an active participant of the movement and had to pay a very heavy price for this participation. Before coming to the events of the rebellion itself, he describes an interesting episode that unfolded in Thrissur in February of that year.[5] On 16 February, the District Magistrate summoned four leading Congressmen. When they refused to give him an undertaking that they would not participate in political agitation, he sent them to jail for five months. A meeting was held

---

[3] EMS, 'A Short History of Peasant Rebellion', p. 180.

[4] Mozhikunnath Brahmadattan Namboodripad, *The Khilafat Reminiscences*, Vatakara: Malabar Institute for Research & Development, originally published in 1965.

[5] Namboodiripad, *The Khilafat Reminiscences*, pp. 21-24.

five days later to honour these leaders for their courage, and some Christians were encouraged by the administration to disrupt the meeting by setting fire to chairs and benches. The day after this, a large 'loyalty' procession was organised by Christians that set fire to several Muslim homes and shops. Hindus and Muslims also mobilised, and there was some stone-throwing. According to Namboodiripad, the government organised 'co-operators, mainly Christians, to attack 'non-co-operators', Hindus and Muslims. As a result, Hindu homes were also attacked.

While many Hindus left Thrissur with their families, their leaders sent telegrams inviting Moplahs from Malabar to come to Thrissur to their aid. The Moplahs poured into the town on 15 March and were provided accommodation at the *Satrum* (rest house) near the Tiruvambadi temple. By nightfall, their numbers increased greatly. All arrangements for their stay and food were made by leaders of the Hindu community. This turn of events forced the administration to broker peace. The Moplahs were requested to return, and railway tickets were purchased for them. Once again, they took out a huge procession in which many Hindus participated, and the entire town echoed with their slogans and shouts.

The immediate response of thousands of Moplahs to the telegrams sent by Thrissur Hindus is proof of the strong bonds between the two communities. Their arrival ensured the failure of the administration's ploy to use Christian loyalists to bring the non-co-operationists in line. It is not surprising that the British administration now did everything in its power to break these bonds of unity between the two groups of non-co-operators.

After this, preparations for the success of Non-Cooperation and Khilafat progressed at a hectic pace. Several conferences were held. M.B.Namboodiripad himself was very active, and, despite the administration's ban orders, he organised the death anniversary meeting of BG Tilak on 1 August in the precincts of his temple.

Muslims and Hindus attended the meeting in large numbers, and this led to his being targeted by the police in the days that followed. Between 20 and 25 August, militant processions shouting the demands for Swaraj and Khilafat were taken out in the area. The administration tried to use strong-arm methods to control them but this only inflamed passions further. Namboodiripad and other Congressmen were active in trying to ensure that the protest remained orderly and peaceful. The arrests, firings, and attacks by the British police and armed forces, however, succeeded in mobilising thousands of Moplahs rallying around leaders like Ali Musaliyar. For a few days, they were successful in ridding a small area around Tirurangadi of the British administration altogether and Ali Musaliyar was crowned king! There were some violent incidents after this in which government treasuries and armouries were looted and the home of the largest landowner was attacked. According to Namboodiripad, this happened because of his pro-British attitude. Some interesting events are described by him. In one, the bank of one Pulloor was raided, and a lot of jewellery pledged there was looted. Another leader of the rebellion, Kunhahmad Haji saw to it that the ornaments were returned (perhaps to those who had pledged them) and Pulloor was compensated. In another incident, a Moplah forcibly retrieved his mortgage document from a Hindu. The Haji threatened the Moplah and ensured that the document was returned. On 25 August, a peace conference was convened at Manjeri by the Haji to guarantee the peace and security of the Hindus.

Efforts were made by several Congressmen to ensure the surrender of the leaders, but Ali Musaliyar and others knew the fate that awaited them and preferred to fight on. Meanwhile, the British called for reinforcements. Their badly planned earlier intervention had led to their withdrawal from the area and had given the rebels the opportunity to establish their own 'rule'. Now they returned determined to crush the rebellion. Ali Musaliyar and his followers had taken shelter in the important Mamram mosque. The British attacked the mosque with bullets. There was some retaliation, but the rebels suffered great losses. Some of them succeeded in escaping and continued the rebellion elsewhere, but Ali Musaliyar surrendered with thirty-seven others. He was sent with many others from Shoranur to Coimbatore jail. Namboodiripad was also a prisoner on this train.

Despite the fact that Namboodiripad had made every effort to ensure peace in his area, he was also arrested on 1 September by the British cavalry. His hands were tied behind his back and the rope that bound him was held by a British soldier on horseback who made him run 20 miles to the Shoranur police station. The torture and humiliation that he suffered continued for several months in several jails. Since arrested Moplahs were also his companions in incarceration, he gives vivid and horrifying descriptions of their sufferings. Several times he says that if he, as a Namboodiripad, was treated so brutally, the treatment meted out to the Moplahs can only be imagined. At this point, Namboodiripad has some words of criticism for the Congress leadership too. He says that neither the State nor the National leaders interceded with the British against the inhuman repression they unleashed in Malabar. Namboodiripad and Ali Musaliyar met again outside the gates of Coimbatore prison, and they had occasion to meet a few times inside the jail. Finally, Ali Musaliyar was hanged in the jail on February 1922.

Soon after Musaliyar's arrest, a curfew was declared in the region, and a reign of terror was unleashed. Thousands were imprisoned and hundreds killed. Each act of repression only increased the Moplahs' determined and militant resistance, which lasted till March 1922. The British resorted to increased and inhuman brutality on the one hand and, on the other, actively sought the help of landlords, mostly Hindus, and numerous agents to help them crush the rebellion in various ways. This, in turn, led to the rebels attacking the Hindus and Muslims who were seen as British agents. Some acts of reprisal were brutal and, innocent people also suffered.

Another prominent leader of the Rebellion was Wariankunnath Kunhammad Haji. He was, and still is revered, as a heroic figure. Namboodiripad had a very good opinion of him. Like Musaliyar, Kunhamad also became the ruler of a 'liberated' area. The historian, Manu Pillai, says about him:

> There is a great deal of oral history and collective memory around him, and Wariankunnath Kunhammad Haji was one of the more prominent leaders of the revolt . . . during the 1921 rebellion, he wrote a letter to *The Hindu*, in which he made it known that reports on forcible conversion were 'entirely untrue', and that these were done by elements linked to the police to vilify the Mappila rebels (he uses the word 'rebels'). Hindus are referred to in this letter are 'brethren', but he does add that those Hindus who helped the military and handed over 'innocent Moplahs' had been 'put to some trouble'. If Hindus were fleeing, it was because the army was evacuating them, whereas he was willing to protect all who came to him, regardless of religious affiliation . . . the leadership of the Mappilas was spread out and fragmented . . . So it is very likely that Kunhamed Haji was being entirely sincere when he put on record that forced conversions were not something his people did, because this may have been the doing of another set . . . The important thing to note is that there were half a dozen leaders and several 'gangs', as the British called them, which sometimes coordinated action, while otherwise sticking to areas under their control. Their policies, outlook, and methods did not always match. When we say 'the Mappilas' we forget sometimes that this was not one solid mass working like a battalion; it was more chaotic. In any case, Kunhamed Haji

does appear a great deal in the report the government put out a year after the rebellion, where he is described as 'the most important leader' and the 'chief rebel leader' . . . Kunhamed Haji appears repeatedly attacking the police, seizing arms, and disappearing, usually with 200 odd men; in January 1922, by which time it was clear the rebellion was failing, this dwindled to 80 'tired and hungry' men till he was finally captured with 21 supporters.[6]

What is not disputed is Haji's heroic death. This is part of British records too. After his capture, he was brutally tortured. Then the British made him an offer: if he apologised, he would be deported to Mecca. The Haji replied that although he loved Mecca, he preferred to die on his own soil. He was shot by a firing squad that he insisted on facing with his eyes uncovered.

Comrade Moyarath Sankaran describes in terrible detail the atrocities committed on the Moplahs by the British army and police and also the role played by the British administration in sowing communal feelings of suspicion, fear, and hatred among Hindus and Muslims. He also describes with admiration the courage and fearlessness of the Moplah rebels which, he says, 'brought honour to Kerala'.[7] According to him, 'Around 8000 Muslims died in the struggle. Nearly 10,000 others were sentenced to five years to life imprisonment in Bellary camp jail. Nearly every day, ten to twenty Muslims were hanged to death during that period . . . nearly 2,000 mutineers were hanged in South Indian jails. Besides, more than 5,000 people were reported missing'.[8] He describes in harrowing detail the way in which the Moplah prisoners were taken to jail to Coimbatore, Vellore and Bellary. He writes 'Once when Manjeri Ramayyer was travelling . . . he heard distress cries from a closed

[6] Soumya Rajendra, 'Variyamkunnath and nuances of the Malabar Rebellion: Author Manu S. Pillai interview', *The News Minute*, 24 June 2020.

[7] Moyarath Sankaran, *Autobiography of a Freedom Fighter and Martyr*, p. 143.

[8] Moyarath Sankaran, *Autobiography of a Freedom Fighter and Martyr*, p. 145.

coach. When the train pulled up at the station . . . he got the coach opened . . . That coach meant to carry only five to eight cows, had 160 men packed into it! Twenty-two men died, forty-five were unconscious.'[9] Comrade Moyarath Sankaran states unambiguously that 'The characterisation of the 1921 peasant struggle as Mappila Riots and as Hindu-Muslim clash has been one of the gravest errors in the history of 20th century Kerala.'[10]

It is imperative that a complete history of this struggle be published so that these errors can be corrected. It is also important that a factual study be available to counter the attempts being made by the Sangh Parivar today to use unfortunate and tragic incidents that occurred in the course of the movement to further their own agenda of destroying social unity.

I will end this inadequate attempt to explain a complex chapter of the freedom struggle in Malabar on a personal note. I became aware of the complexity of this rebellion when I was told about certain events that had taken place in my own family home and village. My great grandmother, A.V. Ammukutty Amma, a landowning matriarch, lived alone in her tharavad (Nair joint family home) in Anakara in Malabar, a few miles away from the epicentre of the rebellion. Her village had a very large population of Moplahs, and many of them worked as tenants on her land. When news of violent attacks started coming in, she thought of leaving Anakara for Chennai. Two of her tenants, Mamykutty and his brother, came to her and asked if she had decided to leave. When she said that she was thinking about it, they put their headcloths at her feet and said that if she went, it would mean that she had lost faith in them. She was a strong, courageous woman and decided to stay. Throughout those days of turmoil and tales of horror, Mamykutty and his brother stayed in the house, sleeping outside her room. A Nair woman, alone in her house, protected by two Moplah men!

<hr>

[9] Moyarath Sankaran, *Autobiography of a Freedom Fighter and Martyr*, p. 150.
[10] *Moyarath Sankaran, Autobiography of a Freedom Fighter and Martyr*, p. 148.

The Moplahs of Anakara and neighbouring villages held a meeting in the mosque. They drafted a letter to the Moplahs of Nilambur and other areas affected by the rebellion requesting them not to cross the Bharatapuzha river and come into their part of Malabar. They said that they had no quarrel with the Hindus there and wished to live in peace.